Huntington Century

The Jewel City
1900-1999

STEPHEN H. PROVOST

Century Cities Publishing 2021
A division of Dragon Crown Books
Martinsville, Virginia   ◆   Fresno, California
San Luis Obispo, California
All rights reserved

ISBN-13: 978-1-949971-25-5

Century Cities

Century Cities Publishing was created to celebrate and preserve the history of midsized and smaller American cities during the 20th century. Narratives are presented in timeline form, drawing on major milestones and lesser-known stories from 1900 to 1999. From athletic champions to retail milestones, from city leaders to entertainers, these books provide a panoramic overview of vibrant, growing cities as they came into their own.

Books in this series

Huntington Century, 2021

Charleston Century, 2021

Roanoke Century, 2021

Danville Century, 2021

Fresno Century, 2021

San Luis Obispo Century, 2021

Cambria Century, 2021

Contents

1   1900–1909: Courting Success   5

2   1910–1919: Budding Metropolis   19

3   1920–1929: Roaring into the Twenties   45

4   1930–1939: Flood of Troubles   73

5   1940–1949: Fires and Marshall   91

6   1950–1959: Huntington at its Peak   109

7   1960–1969: Civil Rights and Blue Laws   135

8   1970–1979: A City in Mourning   151

9   1980–1989: Rise of the Herd   163

10   1990–1999: Gridiron Supremacy   173

"Towns change; they grow or diminish, but hometowns remain as we left them."

Jayne Anne Phillips,
Novelist

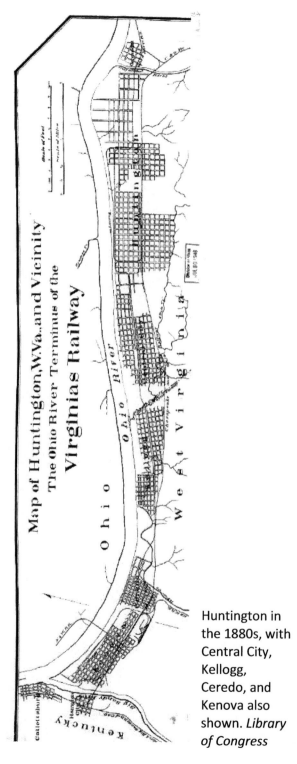

Huntington in the 1880s, with Central City, Kellogg, Ceredo, and Kenova also shown. *Library of Congress*

Introduction

A book on Huntington was the natural next step after my book on Charleston — except it's being released first.

I set out to write a book on Charleston, but then decided to travel west while I was doing my research and explore Huntington, as well. I found a city rich in history and filled with interesting sights, all of which quickly crystallized into the material for this book.

Collis P. Huntington

There aren't any truly big cities in West Virginia, but Huntington and Charleston are the two biggest. They're both actually middle-sized cities, and they've both seen their populations decline in the past 70 years or so, but that doesn't mean they've gotten any less interesting.

Huntington, like many American cities, started off as a railroad town on a river. In this case, the railroad was the C&O, short for Chesapeake and Ohio, and the waterway was the Ohio River.

Huntington wound up being built where it is because Collis P. Huntington, chose it as the place for the C&O's western terminus. He also gave the city its name.

Huntington is notable for many reasons. It was the site of the easternmost bank robbed by the James-Younger Gang and it's home to the state's largest mall, the Huntington Mall. Marshall University, located near the center of town, has drawn headlines for winning national championships and for a tragic plane crash that took the lives of the football team and everyone else on board in 1970.

NASCAR greats raced at a track just west of town on the Grand National circuit, and Camden Park — the state's largest amusement park — has drawn families from around the Tri-State area (where West Virginia, Ohio, and Kentucky meet) for more than a century.

Huntington is a city with contemporary achievements to brag about as well as tales to tell from its pioneer days. *Huntington Century* is the story of what happened in between.

Courting Success

1900–1909

The Cabell County Courthouse was dedicated in 1901. *Author photo*

1900

Milestones

A new century, a new census. Huntington had grown modestly during the 1890s, from just over 10,000 people to nearly 12,000, but the biggest growth was yet to come during the next five decades — and specifically during the next 10 years.

Transportation

The Ohio Valley Electric Railway began operations, connecting Huntington with Ashland, Kentucky, and changing its name to the

Camden Interstate Railway Company.

The company would revert back to its original name in 1908, and streetcar operations would come to an end in 1937.

1901

Government

The Cabell County Courthouse, designed by Kansas City architects Gunn and Curtis, was dedicated on 4th Avenue. It had been in the works since the cornerstone was laid in 1899.

The building, constructed from Berea sandstone and with a copper roof, didn't appear exactly as it looks today, though. King Lumber Company added the west wing in 1923 at a cost of just under $134,000, and Engstrom and Wynn of Wheeling built the east wing and jail in 1938 at a total cost of $454,000.

1902

Football

Marshall College didn't have a head coach, but that didn't seem to matter. The team allowed just two points in seven games (two of them scoreless ties), outscoring their opponents 65-2 while compiling a 5-0-2 record.

Games in those early years were played on what was then called Central Field, now known as the Campus Commons.

Worth noting: All of the team's opponents were high schools from the Tri-State area. College football in the early 20th century was nothing like what it would become.

1903

Community

Andrew Carnegie had a penchant for funding libraries.

The tycoon paid for 1,689 of them to be built in the United States between 1883 and 1929, and one of those went up in Huntington in 1903.

A local architect named James B. Stewart designed the façade, with a central pavilion flanked by Ionic columns. Carnegie donated $35,000 to make it happen.

The Carnegie Library, top, and its cornerstone, laid in 1902, above. The building, completed in 1903, now houses Huntington Junior College. *Author photos*

The Big Dipper at Camden Park. *Author photo*

Recreation

To West Virginians, Camden Park is Disneyland. It's the only amusement park in the state, located on U.S. 60 five miles west of town, just before you get to Ceredo.

It was originally developed as a picnic area by the Camden Interstate Railway in 1903 to boost traffic on its trolley line. The company built it on the site of an Adena tribal burial mound, the third-largest in the state, and some believe it's haunted by Native American spirits.

The park hosted Sunday baseball games early in its history and has been the site of events ranging from dance marathons to roller derbies, from fairs to flagpole sitting.

At first, the only ride there was a carousel at the end of the trolley line. A rollercoaster was added in 1912, and a swimming pool was in operation by 1913.

By 1948, the park had swings, a "whip" ride, Ferris wheel, merry-go-round, airplane rides, small railroad, boats, ponies, a couple of small children's rides, a softball field, and a skating rink to go with the rollercoaster.

A couple of years later, J.P. Boylin bought the park and began adding other attractions. Among them, the Big Dipper rollercoaster, which replaced the original 1912 ride in 1958 and is one of the oldest wooden coasters of its kind still in operation. There was even a zoo in the park, but it was removed during the seventies.

The Day & Night Building was named for a bank that kept its doors open weekdays until 10 p.m. *Author photo*

Business

A five-story building went up at the southeast corner of 10th Street and 4th Avenue that soon came to be known as the Day & Night Building after an early tenant.

The Day & Night Bank didn't keep traditional banker's hours. Instead of closing at 3 p.m., it stayed open all the way until 10 o'clock. Hence the name of the bank — and the building. The

Huntington National Bank took over in 1919, but the building kept its name until the 1950s, when it started being called the Ritter Building.

1905

Cinema

Huntington's first movie theater, Dreamland, opened on the southwest corner of 9th Street and 4th Avenue.

Others followed.

Wonderland on 3rd Avenue opened the next year, with White City on 9th Street, and Fairyland and Gem, both on 3rd Avenue, two years after that.

Most of these new movie houses came and went quickly. They weren't palatial, but rather intimate settings that were often out of business within the space of a year. But that doesn't mean they weren't popular.

In fact, these nickelodeons, as they were often called (because admission cost a nickel), opened at such a high rate that there were 3,000 of them by 1907, just two years after the first one opened in Pittsburgh.

An old skating rink on 4th Avenue between 8th and 9th streets was converted into a cinema called the Lyric in 1910, and by 1916, there were nine movie houses listed in the city directory. In 1914, nationwide, 27 percent of Americans were going to the movies once a week.

Golf

The Spring Valley Country Club opened on Spring Valley Road amid rolling hills in western Huntington. The 18-hole course was the focal point of the club, which also included tennis courts and a swimming pool. It closed in 2008.

Industry

Charles Heiner was 8 years old when he moved from Ironton, Ohio, to Huntington, and he was just 15 when he began working as an apprentice at Schneider's Bakery.

After seven years there, he went out on his own and started baking bread, rolls, pies, and buns out of a room in the Central City Hotel at 12th Street and Adams Avenue. He and his wife Kate sold them door to door.

Four years after they started the business, they moved into their own building and began delivering their baked goods via a horse-drawn wagon.

The company grew from there, with the building eventually covering a full city block. A fleet of trucks made deliveries up to 250 miles away, with distribution reaching warehouses in Virginia, Kentucky, and Ohio.

Heiner's was West Virginia's last family-owned bakery when Earthgrains of St. Louis purchased it in 1996.

1906

Recreation

Joseph Gallick, described as "a well-known theatrical man of Huntington," was set to oversee the opening of Camden Park and had arranged for "a variety of summer amusements."

Lodging

"The greatest building project ever begun in Huntington" (or so it was described in the press) was now finished. The Frederick Hotel opened its doors at 4th Avenue and 10th Street.

Some 3.5 million bricks had been set in place for a project that cost $400,000. An astonishing 282 *miles* of electrical wire helped connect 4,000 lights. In addition to 150 guest rooms, the hotel — described as the finest between Cincinnati and Pittsburgh — provided guests and visitors with a host of amenities.

They included a Turkish bath, billiard parlor, bar, barbershop, and two restaurants, plus 11 private dining rooms. Retail shops served customers at street level.

The Frederick eventually closed as a hotel in 1973.

The Hotel Frederick opened in 1906. *Author photo*

The Hotel Frederick, with the West Virginia Building in the background. *Author photo*

1907

Retail

J.W. Valentine was out as a partner at one Huntington department store, and Eugene Anderson of Portsmouth was in, creating the Anderson-Newcomb Co., capitalized at $125,000.

The business had started back in 1894 as Valentine's dry goods store on 9th Street, and W.H. Newcomb had joined the business a year later; together, Newcomb and Valentine had moved to a larger three-story brick building on 3rd Avenue in 1902.

But now Valentine was bowing out, and Anderson was taking his place... and the store would continue to grow.

In 1913, the partners built a three-story annex, then added three more floors to the main structure in 1920. The company outlasted competitors like Deardorff-Sisler and Morrison's. It was an innovator: the city's first store with a switchboard and the first to install a passenger elevator. Sales were passed from clerk to cashier using a pneumatic tube system.

By 1953, when a fire caused smoke and water damage to the store, it was the city's largest — and it wasn't done growing yet. The owners would construct a two-story addition in 1954 and would stay in business until 1996, although the store was purchased by Stone & Thomas of Wheeling in 1970 and converted to that nameplate a decade later.

Transportation

A new truss bridge was built over the Guyandotte River on 3rd Avenue. As of 1912, the bridge accommodated pedestrians as well as a trolley run by the Ohio Valley Electric Railway.

1909

Community

Central City residents voted to be annexed by Huntington.

Journalism

Huntington in the early 20th century had three different newspapers, but they had plenty in common over the years. *The Herald* and *The Advertiser* had been rivals in the 19th century. A printer named Joseph Harvey Long purchased *The Herald* in 1893, then sold it and bought *The Advertiser* a year later.

Why the switch?

This was an era when newspapers were heavily political. In many towns, two rival newspapers emerged, one espousing Republican values and the other supporting the Democratic agenda. (Some even called themselves *The Republican* or *The Democrat*.) Long was a Democrat, but he had just bought the

Republican-aligned paper. So he sold it and purchased the Democratic-leaning *Advertiser* instead.

Floyd Chapman went in the other direction. The future mayor of Huntington briefly served as city editor of *The Advertiser* starting in 1902, but soon resigned to lead *The Herald's* newsroom.

In 1904, he moved again: This time, though, he started his own newspaper, *The Dispatch*. It lasted only five years before merging with Chapman's previous newspaper to create The *Herald-Dispatch*.

That brings us to 1909.

But it's not the end of the story.

Huntington was a two-paper town again, with Dave Gideon running *The Herald-Dispatch* and publishing his paper in the morning, while Long put out *The Advertiser* in the afternoon.

In the early twenties, *The Advertiser* moved into a new building at 10th Street and 5th Avenue. *The Herald-Dispatch*, meanwhile, built its own new office just down the street. But it only stayed there a short time.

That's because the two rival newspapers merged in 1927 under the name Huntington Publishing Co., with Long as chairman and Gideon as president.

Separate buildings were no longer needed, so *The Herald-Dispatch* moved into *The Advertiser*'s digs. Although the newspapers were now under the same ownership, however, they remained rivals.

It was *The Herald-Dispatch*, however, that survived.

Both newspapers continued to publish for several decades before they were sold in a package deal to Gannett in 1972. In the seventies, however, many afternoon newspapers were losing subscriptions and either converting to a morning format or ceasing publication. So, in the summer of 1979, *The Advertiser* published its last edition.

After nearly a century, Huntington was a one-newspaper town.

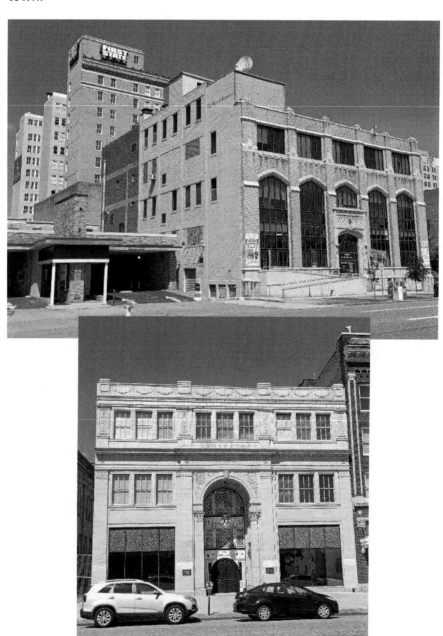

These two buildings both housed the Huntington Herald-Dispatch. *Author photos*

Recreation

The Camden Park Amusement Company was issued a $50,000 charter from the state "for the purpose of building and operating parks for public amusement."

Camden Park was already hosting games for a semi-pro baseball team that the *Charleston Advocate* declared had built "a deserved reputation in the baseball world." Talk of a new pro league was circulating, with Parkersburg, Charleston, and Wheeling mentioned as other potential team sites.

There was also speculation that Huntington might join the Ohio State League, which included a team in Portsmouth, just a short distance away.

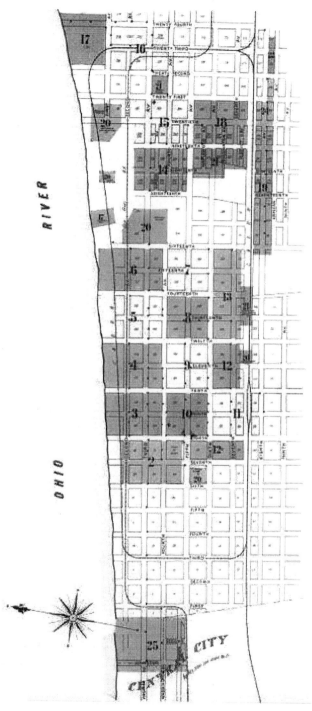

Sanborn Fire Insurance map of Huntington, 1904.
Library of Congress

Budding Metropolis

1910–1919

The Huntington Bank and Trust Building, constructed in 1910, was later home to Guaranty Bank and Trust and, most recently, Union Bank.

1910

Baseball

Huntington had its first pro team in organized baseball, making its debut in the Virginia Valley League.

The Blue Sox played weekday games in the new 4,500-seat League Park on Ohio Street and 8th Street, right on the Ohio River, and played Sundays in Camden Park.

Huntington was the class of the six-team Class-D circuit, finishing first with a record of 61-42. (Charleston actually won more games, but also lost more and therefore had a lower winning percentage.)

The manager of the Huntington team was listed as Cy Young, but it wasn't the Hall of Fame pitcher, who was still throwing in the big leagues — for Cleveland — at the time. It was Julius Carl Young, nicknamed Cy.

But he didn't last the full campaign.

Albert "Dutch" Nazel took over at midseason and guided the team to the pennant on the strength of two impressive pitchers. George Baumgardner, a native of nearby Barboursville, made the jump all the way to the majors the following season. He played five seasons with the St. Louis Browns, posting a career-best 16-14 record in 1914.

Frank Nicholson, the Blue Sox's No. 2 pitcher, went up to the majors briefly in 1912, too, although he pitched in just a couple of games with the Phillies.

Perhaps the league's biggest star was Benny Kauff, who played in Parkersburg and compiled a batting average that was at least .336 and could have been as high as .417, depending on the source. Three years later, Kauff would sign on with the newly minted third major league, the Federal League, where he would win two batting titles in as many years.

The VVL had its own set of baseball cards, which were packaged with cigarettes in those days. According to the *Point Pleasant Register*, hometown newspaper of the third-place team:

"The members of the different teams in the Virginia Valley League will be well known in a few days, especially by the cigarette smokers, and to a large number of youngsters who save the pictures from cigarette packages.

"The manufacturers of a grade of cigarettes have asked for the pictures of the players in the different teams in the league and they will put them [the pictures, not the players] in the packages of cigarettes. The different teams have been posing for the camera the last few days."

Business

The Huntington Bank and Trust building opened on 9th Street between 5th and 6th Avenues. The first floor of the new high rise housed the bank and a coffee shop, but the high-rise also included 175 office spaces.

It was state-of-the-art for its day, with amenities like hot and cold water in every room, combination locks in every office, ice water fountains on every floor, a vacuum steam system, and fireproof vaults.

The bank would fail during the Depression, and other banks would occupy the building after that: the Guaranty Bank and Trust, First Sentry Bank, and most recently, United Bank.

Milestones

Huntington had nearly tripled in size over the past 10 years. It had barely been bigger than Charleston in 1900, but it was now substantially larger at 31,161 compared with the state capital's 22,996 — even though Charleston, too, had seen significant growth.

Huntington had added nearly 20,000 people in a single decade, a 161.4 percent increase that gave it a population of 31,161 to start the new decade. But it wasn't the state's largest city: That honor belonged to Wheeling up north, which had topped the 41,000 despite seeing slower growth.

Lodging

The 100-room Fifth Avenue Hotel went up at 5th Avenue and 9th Street, the site originally occupied by the First Congregational Church.

The three-story brick building, with retail shops along 9th Street, was built by Hansford Watts, a former deputy U.S. marshal who already co-owned the Adelphi Hotel at 6th Avenue and 9th Street, and also owned a jewelry store in Ashland, Kentucky.

The hotel added 30 more rooms at a cost of $25,000 in 1917 and was the original home to Bailey's Cafeteria, which operated in the basement. Later, in the 1980s, an eatery called Snaks Fifth Avenue operated there, but the hotel closed not long after that.

1911

Baseball

The Virginia Valley League changed its name to the Mountain States League, and the Huntington Blue Sox were keen on defending their championship.

Dutch Nazel was back at the helm, and both George Baumgardner and Frank Nicholson were back with the team (they wouldn't be called up to the majors until after the MSL season ended). They both made a big impact again: Baumgardner led the league in wins and winning percentage with a 24-9 record, and Nicholson won 16 more games.

The Blue Sox, led at the plate by Kemper Shelton's .331 batting average, won the first-half title but didn't fare as well after the midway point, finishing 60-53 overall. If everything had gone according to plan, they would have faced off against second-half champion Montgomery, which finished with the best overall record. But it didn't turn out that way.

With Middleport-Pomeroy having finished just a game behind Montgomery in the second-half race, a protested game between Montgomery and Charleston threw everything up in the air. The National Association of Professional Baseball Leagues gave Charleston the victory, which in turn gave Middleton-Pomeroy the second-half title.

The playoffs, however, were canceled, robbing Huntington of a shot at the title.

The Blue Sox and the league returned in 1912, but financial woes destroyed it before the season could be completed. Charleston dropped out July 1, and Huntington and Ashland-Catlettsburg both folded a week later, leaving just three teams in operation and causing the entire league to disband. Huntington concluded the abbreviated season with a 27-20 record.

Community

Residents from Guyandotte, a community at the confluence of the Ohio and Guyandotte rivers that dated back to the early 19th century, voted to be annexed by Huntington.

1912

Health Care

C.C. Barnett, a medical doctor trained at Howard University, had already been practicing for a decade in Huntington, treating the African-American patients as both a doctor and a surgeon.

The Barnett Hospital and Nursing School is an apartment complex today. *Author photo*

Barnett's first wife died in 1909, and he married a nurse named Clara B. Matthews in 1912. Around that time, he heard about the death of a young Black man who had been injured while working for the Chesapeake & Ohio Railway and had died after he was refused treatment because of his race.

The incident inspired him to open up the Barnett Hospital in his home. From just a few beds initially, it grew to a 50-bed facility that employed 10 physicians and eight nurses. There were two operating rooms and an X-ray department, and in 1918, Clara Barnett opened the Barnett Nursing School.

A year after it was established, the *Savannah Tribune* lauded the Barnett Hospital as the most modern private hospital in Huntington.

And the *Journal of the National Medical Association* declared that a "number of surgeons who have had training in some of the great hospitals of this country and Europe, have started excellent private hospitals, where they not only have an opportunity to gain experience from the wealth of clinical material, but it gives the colored people a chance to get expert treatment from surgeons and clinicians of their own race. [A] brilliant example of this [is] Dr. C.C. Barnett, Huntington."

Barnett lost his mortgage on the hospital during the Depression, but the city operated it as an integrated facility until it closed in 1939. Starting in 1947, it housed the offices of a labor union, and more recently has been used for apartments.

Prohibition

West Virginia voters cast their ballots, and the results were decisive: They'd had enough of alcohol. Statewide prohibition passed by a margin of nearly 75,000 votes — and ministers in Huntington couldn't have been more pleased.

"It was a moral triumph and the greatest victory ever won in a temperance campaign," enthused L.L. Wood, pastor of Fifth Avenue Baptist Church, predicting: "It will have a far-reaching influence, in fact, a national effect."

Of course, he turned out to be right: National Prohibition passed less than nine years later.

In West Virginia, though, the process didn't take effect immediately. Saloons had until July 1, 1914 to close up shop.

Many bar owners simply relocated to adjacent states, while breweries converted their plants to other uses, such as storage houses and ice plants.

When the date to go dry arrived, Huntington saloons did so without incident.

A dispatch in the *Fairmont West Virginian* described the day prohibition took effect: "No disorder marked the last days of the saloon in Huntington. The prohibition amendment went into effect at midnight, but long before the hour had struck many places were out of business, their stocks gone, their bars dismantled and their signs obliterated."

In all, 30 saloons and a brewery went out of business. And the move was a costly one, both to the businesses and to the government. The liquor stock alone was valued at $250,000, and the value of the saloon business, not counting the brewery, at half a million.

Revenues to state and local governments would go down, too, by roughly $30,000 a year each. But fines for violating the law were designed to replenish the state's coffers.

Liquor was defined broadly to include "all malt, vinous or spiritous liquors, wine, porter, ale, beer, or any other intoxicating drink, mixture or preparations and mixtures which will produce intoxication, and all beverages containing as much as one-half of one per centum of alcohol by volume shall be deemed spirituous liquors."

And it wasn't just the sale of liquor that was banned, but possessing it, as well. A first offense would cost you $100 to $500 in fines, which would be somewhere between $2,600 and $13,300 in 2021 dollars. That's not cheap in anyone's book.

But that doesn't mean you couldn't get alcohol in Huntington. You just had to know where to look. Your best bet would have been "The Strip," a seedy section of 4th Avenue between 10th and 11th streets that housed a line of speakeasies, brothels, and gambling parlors.

You could find bootlegged whiskey at the Crescent Pool Hall or buy a drink at an apartment above the State Theater.

Retail

The Deardorff-Sisler Company received a charter to conduct business, the new owners advertising themselves as "successors to the Valentine-Crow Co." The department store was open by

November at 10th Street and 4th Avenue, offering women's and juniors coats and suits for $15 and up.

"Such tempting prices! Such handsome models! Such beautiful cloths, three striking qualities thrown together to make the most forcible," a newspaper ad enthused. "A glance will convince you — see for yourself."

By 1917, the business had relocated to a three-story building on the 400 block of 9th Street, the site of the recently demolished old city hall, and was describing itself as Huntington's style center and largest department store. Hours were 8:30 a.m. to 6 p.m. daily and 9:30 to 6 on Saturdays.

1913

Baseball

The Huntington Blue Sox were without a home, but the situation was just temporary.

Joe Carr, secretary-treasurer of the Ohio State League, was in charge of reorganizing that circuit, and he invited both Huntington and Charleston to join, along with teams from Lexington and Maysville in Kentucky. If Carr's name is familiar, it's probably because he also owned a professional football team called the Columbus Panhandles.

In 1921, he would become president of the National Football League, a position he'd retain until 1939.

Pitcher Al Mamaux was the most prominent player on the Blue Sox during their first year in the new league, finishing the season with an 18-16 record. Huntington could only manage a fourth-place showing with a 68-68 record, but Mamaux was destined for greater things. He would pitch the next 12 seasons in the majors, including consecutive 21-win seasons for the Pittsburgh Pirates in 1915 and 1916.

The Blue Sox would never find much success in the Ohio State League, which itself would come to an end after the 1916 season. For the 15 years that followed, Huntington baseball would exist only in city leagues; organized pro ball would have to wait until 1931.

Community

Back in 1908, Huntington purchased 55 acres of land around Four Pole Creek to build a new city incinerator. But timber magnate Charles Ritter didn't like the idea of an incinerator downhill below his estate, so he came up with a different proposal: He'd deed an additional 20 acres of land to the city on the condition that the land become a park instead.

Mayor Rufus Switzer embraced the idea, and Ritter Park was soon a reality on 8th Street.

The 75-acre park, with a garden of 3,300 roses and winding footpath would be named one of the 10 best public spaces in America by the American Planning Association nearly a century later in 2012.

But it wasn't always so picturesque. At one point, it featured a manmade pond called Lake Chaposcane, a nonsensical name composed of two letters from the name of each city commissioners who was serving at the time. Its muddy waters ultimately had to be drained after a child drowned there.

There were other, less serious problems, too. Soon after the park opened, it became a location of choice for lovebirds.

The *Fairmont West Virginian* reported that the "annual spooning season," created a "vexing question" for city commissioners that was "one of the paramount issues in Huntington."

The commissioners, determined to do battle with the lovestruck denizens of their fair city, installed chair-like benches just big enough for one person. But they seemed to have overlooked the possibility that couples could simply push the benches together.

Undeterred by this setback, the city leaders installed a large number of electric lights to throw a spotlight on the "lover's lanes" and "cozy nooks" where the spooners sought refuge. According to the *West Virginian*, these lights made the park as bright by night as it was during the day.

The newspaper concluded: "This will no doubt relieve the situation unless some daring Adonis finds the switch and turns off the current."

Disaster

The Ohio River took a bite out of Huntington — and the city's economy.

The river's waters spilled over into a large residential area near the C&O Railway at both the eastern and western ends of the city. Its rail yards and repair shops were badly damaged and were forced to close temporarily, putting 2,000 skilled laborers out of work.

Nearly every factory sustained some damage, and only one of the eight to 10 banks in town remained open in the days following the deluge. Most of the city was reduced to seeing by lantern and candlelight.

The businesses on 2nd, 3rd, and 4th avenues took the "full force of the overflow," the *Hinton Daily News* reported. A photo taken on 3rd Avenue showed rowboats making their way up the street beneath arches of electric lights, past an undertaker, shoe store, carpeting store, and five-and-dime.

In fact, every street in the business section was flooded for a stretch of two or three blocks, creating what the newspaper called "necks of water on a level with and leading to the rampant Ohio."

Some sections of street were under as much as 20 feet of water, and hundreds of houses were so deeply submerged that nothing more than their roofs were showing.

Twenty-thousand people were homeless, with a thousand families camped in tents on a mountainside near Guyandotte. One man took his own life rather than risk being taken by the waters. William Sullivan had been marooned on the second floor of his home with his wife and seven children. They had been rescued, but he had been left behind because there wasn't room in the rescuers' boat.

Fearing they wouldn't return for him, he committed suicide rather than risk being drowned.

Store owners were ruined, or close to it.

J.P. Field, owner of a department store called The Fashion, said his stock was almost entirely ruined and he faced a loss of some $40,000. Other merchants had removed some of their goods in time to save them, but the Anderson-Newcomb and Zenner-Bradshaw stores still faced heavy losses. ...

The flood wasn't the only disaster, or the first, to hit Huntington in 1913: On New Year's Day, the C&O Railroad bridge over the Guyandotte River collapsed.

An account of the calamity in the *Hinton Daily News* read like a script from a disaster movie.

"According to eyewitnesses, the bridge went without warning," it began. "The men were caught like rats in a trap and hurled into the turbulent stream. There was no place for escape. Just the cries of the dying men and the crash of griding steel and weed, then oblivion."

It wasn't as though there had been no warning. The bridge had been known to be in perilous condition for weeks and was in the midst of renovations during which it was being held together by temporary supports.

Logjams and rogue timber projectiles had been a problem on the river for years, created when thousands of logs were sent downriver by timber companies. The logs were supposed to be tied together, but when the current became swift, they could become dislodged and careen forward at an alarming rate.

An early postcard shows logs tied together on the Guyandotte River. *Public domain*

Logs had destroyed a previous bridge there in 1906, and its replacement had fallen victim to a wave of logs numbering as many as 125,000. In 1912, more logs had damaged the latest bridge, leading to warnings it wasn't safe.

Several trains crossed it without incident on New Year's Day before a freight train heading from Hinton to Russell, Kentucky (the engineer's hometown), was stopped by flagmen when it got there. Its load of 490,000 pounds was heavier than the others, and several of the 30 workers busy on the bridge left, ostensibly to get material from the bank, intending to return once the locomotive made it across.

Either that, or they were just plain scared.

At 11 a.m., the train made its way onto the bridge and got as far as the middle span before it collapsed. The locomotive, a boxcar, and 13 workers were hurled into the river below, and a crowd of 2,000 people from the city quickly gathered to see what had happened. The engine vanished beneath the river waters.

Seven people (engineer "Shorty" Webber and six bridge workers) were killed, while 15 others were injured; three of the bodies were never recovered. The cost to the railroad: $500,000.

1914

Dining

Lebanese immigrant Mike Thabit opened a restaurant at 3rd Avenue and 8th Street, a business that lasted in one form or another for nearly a century.

Thabit moved into a larger space on 8th Street a few years later, selling homemade candy at his Aster Restaurant and Candy Company. Then, in 1946, he moved for 1117 4th Ave., renaming the eatery simply Thabit's.

Track and Field

Huntington High won the first-ever state track and field meet and would win five of the first six, with only Charleston High breaking the string in 1916.

1915

Basketball

Basketball games were typically low scoring during the first half of the century. There wasn't a shot clock, and the ball was returned to center court for a new tip-off after every basket. Still, this year's state championship lacked offensive punch even by the standards of the day.

Huntington and Wheeling combined for just 32 points, tied for the third-lowest total in state finals history. Huntington prevailed 17-15 to claim the school's first Class A championship, but the game was a barnburner compared to the Class B title game two years earlier, when Keyser beat West Monongah by the eye-popping score of 13-7.

Huntington City Hall. *Author photo*

Community

Huntington built its third city hall, following the original wood-frame building in 1871 and a bigger, sturdier brick structure in 1886. Both were on 9th Street.

For the new city hall, however, leaders chose a plot of land at 8th Street and 5th Avenue. They paid $44,000 — the equivalent of about $1.2 million in 2021 — and that was just for the property; they hadn't even built the building yet.

The structure itself cost $115,000 and included a 2,500-seat auditorium in the center. Verus T. Ritter designed it, one of several projects around town that he drew up, including Huntington High School. The two buildings are similar in some respects, both featuring rectangular lines accented by impressive columns at the entrance in a neoclassical style. ...

While one new monument went up, another came down — mysteriously — and disappeared.

A cast-iron statue of a Union soldier had gone up in the 1890s at 5th Avenue and 9th Street, honoring the state's membership in the Union.

West Virginia had been part of Virginia at the outbreak of the Civil War, but although that state joined the Confederacy, sympathies in the west ran to the Union side. So 39 counties began the process of separating and forming their own state, initially to be called Kanawha.

Still, divisions remained.

After the Union statue went up, a group of Confederate sympathizers sought to have a statue of a rebel soldier put up in Ritter Park as a way to balance things out. This, of course, caused a fierce debate with residents who were proud of their state's allegiance to the Union.

Then, one morning, the Union statue was simply gone. Some folks said they'd seen it loaded into a wagon overnight, but had assumed it was merely being moved to Ritter Park. But it never turned up there — or anywhere else. In fact, it had just been stolen, like a number of other Union monuments that disappeared over the years.

As a result, there wound up being more Confederate

memorials in West Virginia than Union monuments, even though the state not only supported the Union side, but separated from Virginia in order to do so.

Northcott Hall before its demolition. *HABS/Library of Congress*

Education

The second building on Marshall's campus opened to students. Funding had been appropriated two years earlier for Northcott Hall, named for Gustavus A. Northcott, president of the West Virginia Senate.

Before the construction of Northcott Hall, the only building on campus was the original structure known as Old Main, and its additions.

Northcott Hall served as the school's original science building. It was ultimately razed in 1996 to make room for a new library. One of the building's arches was preserved, however, and incorporated in the new Drinko Library.

Football

Marshall scored just one touchdown in a lopsided loss to West Virginia University, but the team made that single score memorable.

Facing a shutout late in the game, Marshall had driven to the WVU 20-yard line when coach Boyd Chambers sent in a trick play the likes of which no one had ever seen. Tailback Bradley Workman faded back to pass, which was rare in itself. Passing plays were rare at the time, but the one Marshall was about to execute was downright bizarre.

Boyd Chambers, coach of the Marshall team who drew up the "tower pass." *Public domain*

Two potential receivers — Dayton "Runt" Carter and Okey "Blondie" Taylor — ran to the same part of the end zone, and Workman heaved the ball in their direction. Carter then executed the "tower pass" by climbing onto Taylor's shoulders and grabbing the ball for six points.

The play was ruled legal at the time, but was outlawed the following year.

The final score: Marshall 6, West Virginia 92.

1916

Cinema

The Orpheum Theatre opened at 1021 4th Ave. downtown in March. Verus T. Ritter of Ritter-Vickers was the architect.

The 1,600-seat theater cost $75,000 to build and opened with a showing of *Peggy*, a movie that featured Broadway actress Billie Burke in her film debut.

The Orpheum Theater during a parade. *Cinema Treasures, Creative Commons 2.0*

Among the early live engagements was the team of Don and Mabel Garrison, who stopped there in 1917 to present two features: "The Girl in the Moon" and "Washington Was a Grand Old Man." Don Garrison was a composer, and the pair had performed in theaters across the country by the time they hit Huntington. They carried their own scenery around with them to augment their singing show.

That same year, the Hyman family — who already operated the Dixie and Lyric theaters in town — began leasing the theater.

The 1937 marquee touted showings of *Portia on Trial* and a comedy called *High Flyers* featuring Bert Wheeler and Robert Woolsey.

In later years, the theater was renamed the Cinema Theatre and converted into a four-plex. It remained open in that form until it closed in late 2011

The Cinema Theatre in 2021. *Author photo*

1917

Industry

Big tobacco was increasing its presence in town, and the result was a financial windfall for Huntington: Liggett and Myers, makers of Chesterfield cigarettes.

The company planned to invest half a million dollars in a new plant in Huntington, which would employ 1,000 workers and make both cigarettes and chewing tobacco.

An addition to the original four-story red brick warehouse building — a two-story warehouse behind it — would be added in 1920. Already on the site was a redrying plant built in 1910.

By 1918, more than 9.55 million pounds of tobacco were sold in West Virginia at a price of 35.47 cents a pound, and the Huntington tobacco market would hit its zenith in the first half of the next decade.

The Liggett and Myers tobacco plant is still standing in Huntington. *Author photo*

Retail

If you were in the market for shoes, you had no shortage of choices on 3rd and 4th avenues: The Bon Ton Boot Shop, J. Broh, the Henry Shoe Co., Smith Shoery, and Watters Shoe Co. were all open for business.

Transportation

Before the 6th Street Bridge was built in 1926, it wasn't easy to get across the Ohio River from Huntington.

You could try to swim.

Or, in 1917, you could take the ferry. That's when Paul Thomas created the 26th Street Ferry Company that launched service from (naturally) 26th Street across the river to Bradrick in Lawrence County, Ohio.

A year later, Ben Flesher invested in an 1887 sternwheeler called the New Pike. He brought the rebuilt ship to town, renamed it the "City of Huntington," and began service from the 10th Street landing to Chesapeake, Ohio.

The boat continued to operate for a decade after the new bridge opened, finally sinking in an icy Symmes Creek, Ohio, in 1936.

The "City of Huntington" ferry plies the waters of the Ohio River in this early postcard. *Author collection*

1918

Lodging

The Hotel Farr, named for its builder, coalman James Farr, was supposed to be 14 stories tall. But World War I pushed the cost of construction up, and Farr had to stop halfway up. It opened in 1918 nonetheless, at seven stories, and remained open at 9th Street and 4th Avenue until 1965.

If the Hotel Farr building looks a little shorter than it should be, that's because it is. *Author photo*

1919

Fire

A bolt of lightning decided to take the elevator at the Morrison Department Store, sparking a fire that swept through Huntington's business district in mid-July.

The strike hit the store's elevator shaft on 4th Avenue, sparking a fire that destroyed the building along with the Dixie Theatre and a law firm's offices. *The Lexington Leader* reported that "flames rose more than a hundred feet in the air, illuminating the entire business section until it was as light as if in the glare of the sun.

"The heat was so intense that it cracked windows across the street and melted huge iron girders."

Lighting struck elsewhere, too, starting other fires at

11th Street and 2nd Avenue, the C&O railway shops, and utility poles at 20th Street and 4th Avenue. Total losses were pegged at $362,000, with Morrison's taking the brunt of the damage — to the tune of a quarter-million dollars.

The business, however, was open again in time for Christmas.

Simms School houses apartments in 2021. *Author photo*

Education

Huntington's school board purchased land for a new building to house the Henry Clay Simms School, which had been open since 1899.

The two-story brick structure with a central colonnade would welcome its first students in 1921, opening the school to a larger enrollment that fluctuated between 300 and 600 in the years ahead.

It closed in 1982 and was eventually added to the National Register of Historic Places.

Football

After taking a year off for World War I, Marshall returned to the football field and posted its best record to date, going unbeaten in eight games. The team's first five opponents (and six of eight overall) failed to score a single point.

Marshall posted wins of 76-0 over Morris Harvey and 65-0 over the Greenbrier Military Academy, outscoring opponents by a combined 302-13 overall on the year.

STEPHEN H. PROVOST

Roaring into the Twenties
1920–1929

The Gideon Building was for many years home to the W.T. Grant discount store, a competitor to Woolworth's. *Author photo*

1920

Milestones

Huntington's population topped the 50,000 mark after a surge of 61 percent in the 1910s. Huntington added more than 19,000 people, but it wasn't the only city seeing an influx of new residents. In fact, this census year saw a national milestone: For the first time, more people lived in U.S. cities than in rural areas.

Charleston added nearly 17,000 people during the decade, and Wheeling remained the state's largest city after a 35 percent surge to more than 56,000. But Wheeling was nearing its peak, and Huntington would soon surpass it.

1923

Health Care

The Huntington Children's Hospital, the only medical facility in the area specifically for sick children, opened in a historic home at 11th Street and 5th Avenue.

The building would be demolished in 1947 and replaced by the Huntington Savings Bank.

Retail

It was the era of the five-and-dime, dominated by stores like Woolworth, Kress, and W.T. Grant. The Grant chain opened a store in Huntington in 1923 in a three-story building at 3rd Avenue and 10th Street that had previously housed Samuel Gideon's clothing store.

Gideon had the building constructed in 1915, but he died eight years later, and the Grant company bought it. At first, Grant shared the ground floor with a women's clothing store called Mangel's, but the discounter eventually took over the entire space.

The store stayed open until 1976, when the chain went out of business.

Several years after Grant opened up shop, a competitor opened up just down the street. H.L. Green was another dime store chain that had a presence in 133 stores by 1935. There was an H.L. Green in Charleston, too.

In Huntington, the Green store lasted longer than Grant or any of the other five-and-dimes: The store was remodeled in 1975 with new flooring, counters, and lighting. After that, it stayed in business for another 17 years before finally closing in 1992.

1924

The Collis P. Huntington statue in front of the C&O Railroad Depot. *Author photo*

Community

If it was good enough for Mount Rushmore, it was good enough for Huntington.

Gutzon Borglum, who would later create the iconic presidents' faces on Mount Rushmore, undertook a much more modest project in 1924 when Collis P. Huntington's widow Arabella and his nephew Henry commissioned him to create a statue of the railroad financier.

Huntington had purchased the C&O Railroad and built a rail line through the Appalachians, with its terminus on the Ohio River.

They called it Huntington in his honor.

The 8-foot-high statue of Huntington was unveiled in October at a ceremony attended by about 7,000 people in front of the C&O Depot, now owned by CSX Transportation. That's where it stands today.

Health Care

The Pallottine Missionary Sisters, who had opened two hospitals in West Virginia — Richwood in 1912 and Buckhannon in 1921 — were invited by the bishop in Wheeling to start a third hospital, in Huntington.

The sisters bought two buildings that had housed a failed prep school and used the smaller one (a former gymnasium) for their convent while turning the larger one into St. Mary's Hospital. It started out with 35 beds, and a three-story addition in 1930 would more than triple its capacity to 110.

Retail

Mr. Peanut once had a permanent home — not just the shelf at your local grocery store.

Planters Peanuts, founded in 1906, actually had its own stores across the country for decades, only closing them in the sixties to focus on supermarket sales. One such store was located on Huntington's 4th Avenue, next to the Keith-Albee Theatre (although it opened four years before the theater did).

Mr. Peanut, a monocled peanut in a top hat introduced by Planters in 1916, greeted pedestrians on the sidewalk by tapping his cane on the glass of the display window.

A year after it opened, the store was connected with the newly completed Huntington Arcade, which featured several shops and business offices. The Keith-Albee no doubt benefitted from the foot traffic drawn to the area by the Peanut Shoppe, but business went the other way, too: Theater patrons often stepped out to buy munchies at the Peanut Shoppe rather than from the theater's concessions.

The Peanut Shoppe stayed in business as an independent store after Planters quit the direct retail business, enduring until it finally closed in 2009. Until then, you could find a lot more than peanuts there. Giant gumballs, almonds, pecans, cashews, Macadamia nuts, gumdrops, chocolate-covered raisins, and even chocolate-covered Double Stuff Oreos were on display.

Street map of Huntington in 1925.

Transportation

The Huntington-Charleston Motor Bus and White Transportation companies had both been serving the area's mass transit needs. But now Arthur Hill combined the two bus companies into a single entity: Midland Trail Transit.

Hill, the former secretary and treasurer of the Charleston Interurban Railroad, knew the transportation business. His new company started running buses between Huntington and Charleston on the road that would soon become U.S. 60 — but was then known only as the Midland Trail. Hence the name.

In 1926, however, the U.S. government paved the way for a dramatic rise in interstate traffic by creating the first federal highway system. The network, with its black-and-white shields, marked an increased commitment to good roads and created a network for travelers to see the country through the windshields of their Model-Ts.

And from the passenger seats of buses.

A sign on 5th Avenue at the intersection of U.S. 60 directs travelers to Barboursville, Proctorville, and Point Pleasant. *Author photo*

The Midland Trail had given Hill access to one of the first transcontinental roads, stretching from the nation's capital west to California. You could travel from West Virginia to places like Louisville, St. Louis, Kansas City, and Denver. But the new U.S. 60 opened up even more territory.

Simply put, the new highway system meant more opportunity, and in 1927, Hill combined his company with three others to expand his territory, changing the name once again. Now known as Blue and Gray Transit (or B&G Lines), the company's buses went from Huntington to places like Charleston and Bluefield in West Virginia, along with Ohio cities like Portsmouth and Columbus, and into Kentucky as well.

In 1929, he and a partner would form the National Highway Transport Company, although it was still referred to as Blue and Gray. The following year, B&G buses traveled 5.1 million miles, the equivalent of 204 trips around the world, and could be seen on highways as far away as Pennsylvania, Illinois, and south to Florida — a dozen states in all. The company adopted the slogan "there's a Blue and Gray going your way," and was seeking to live up to it.

The year 1930 saw the company purchase more than 100 buses, including eight new 33-passenger vehicles and a dozen that fit 21 passengers each. Meanwhile, new terminals were being built and others expanded.

B&G doubled the size of its Portsmouth terminal and completed work at the start of 1930 on a new brick building on 4th Avenue in Huntington. A news account at the time in the Charleston Daily Mail reported:

"The Huntington bus terminal is considered one of the most modern establishments of its kind east of Kansas City. It has a news stand, lunchrooms, restrooms, parlors and has all the necessary facilities for conveniently loading 10 buses at the same time."

Drivers and dispatchers wore light gray uniforms with belts and leggings around the ankles. The uniforms were awarded "in recognition of efficiency in operating buses" and for employees not "having any accidents chargeable to them during a 12-months period."

B&G would become part of the Greyhound system as Atlantic Greyhound in 1931.

1925

Business

The Coal Exchange Building rose 160 feet and 14 stories high, a $1.2 million investment in Huntington that was home to the Coal Exchange Bank.

The bank itself only lasted eight years before it fell victim to the Depression and the building was sold at auction to the C&O Railroad. Later, Kaiser Drug Store moved in on the bottom floor, and a parade of other businesses came and went. The building, seen lit up below on a Tichnor Brothers postcard, still stands at 11th Street and 4th Avenue.

The Coal Exchange Building, later known as the C&O Railway Building, rises 14 stories above Huntington at the corner of 11th Avenue. A number of businesses have occupied the ground floor over the years, including Glenn's Sporting Goods, pictured here in 2021. *Author photo*

Two views of the Palace Theatre, the lower one seen in the 1960s or early '70s. *elmorovivo and TallPallInKy, Cinema Treasures, Creative Commons 2.0*

Cinema

With 1,300 seats, the Palace Theatre opened Nov. 25 as a new rival to the Orpheum downtown at 1030 4th Ave.

The theater, nestled between Morgan's and the Becker Music Store (later Carpet Barn), was eventually purchased by Greater Huntington Theatres and renamed the two-screen Camelot. It closed its doors in 2006 and found new life as the Jeslyn Performing Arts Center when it reopened.

Fire

Times were good at Zenner-Bradshaw, and the department store was getting ready for the Christmas season. In November, the store added a large show window to display its best merchandise and a bargain basement to attract shoppers looking for a deal. A new toy department was added, too, just in time for holiday shopping.

The store had stocked up on merchandise just for Christmas and anticipated strong revenues.

But Christmas never arrived at the majestic two-story building on 4th Avenue, built in the style of a Roman temple. Early on the morning of Dec. 16, a fire broke out at the business and 60 firefighters rushed to the scene, waking up guests at the Florentine and Frederick hotels to evacuate them as a crowd gathered to watch the flames.

By the time it was all over, only the building's front wall was left. The store lost $250,000 worth of merchandise and $400,000 in total damage.

The store never reopened, but George Bradshaw moved over to competitor McMahon-Diehl, where he became president and ultimately changed the name to Bradshaw-Diehl.

The Keith-Albee Theatre would go up three years later on the site once occupied by Zenner-Bradshaw.

Bradshaw-Diehl, meanwhile, would stay open on 3rd Avenue until 1971.

Football

An independent in previous years, Marshall College joined the West Virginia Athletic Conference. Players had to be enrolled at Marshall in order to qualify for competition and had to pass at least 12 hours per semester.

Marshall promptly won the championship in its first year, going 3-0-2 in conference play and 4-1-4 overall (all four ties came in a four-game stretch during the middle of the season.)

The team's most lopsided victory was a 58-2 homefield win over Morris Harvey on Nov. 14, but the season ended with a nonconference loss to Louisville, 7-2.

Prohibition

Raids by federal agents near Camden Park resulted in 10 arrests and the seizure of 45 gallons of moonshine whiskey.

Retail

Lebanese immigrant Toufeek Abu Nasser founded the Art Linen Shop at 316 9th St. It stayed open for 23 years at that location before he moved across the street. Having expanded the store's merchandise to include women's sportswear and lingerie, and children's clothing, he renamed the business Nasser's Department Store.

There he added a bridal salon and other departments and stayed open 35 more years before selling the store in 1983. He died 12 years later at the age of 96.

1926

Two views of
Frederick
Douglass High
School.
Author photo

Education

A new building was completed for Frederick Douglass School on 10th Street.

The school was established in 1891 in a brick building at 8th Avenue and 16th Street. Its early graduates included Carter G. Woodson, who also served as the school's principal. He would go on to become the second Black American to earn a Ph.D. from Harvard and later became so influential in the field of African-American history that he became known as the Father of Black History.

Woodson founded Negro Heritage Week, later known as Black History Week and a forerunner of Black History Month.

"Those who have no record of what their forebears have accomplished lose the inspiration which comes from the teaching of biography and history," Woodson said.

So he set out to change that.

The school, meanwhile, set out to change the lives of Huntington teenagers, but it faced challenges: Heading into the 20th century, enrollment was growing to the point that expansion became a necessity. Two rooms were added in 1905, and a two-story addition with 10 rooms followed in 1913 at a cost of $40,000. It included a library, office, chemistry and physics lab, and sewing room.

But despite these expansions, by 1919, the school's enrollment was up to 120 just at the high school, and the building housed grades 1-12.

It was clear a larger building was needed. The new three-story, red brick campus on 10th Street accommodated both senior and junior high students. The old building, meanwhile, became an elementary school named for C.C. Barnett, the doctor who had founded Barnett Hospital. It was torn down in 1994.

Ira De Augustine Reid, a noted sociologist who taught at

Atlanta University, New York University, and Haverford College, also taught social science at Douglass High for a year. And Basketball Hall of Famer Hal Greer starred at Douglass in the 1950s.

The second Douglass campus closed as a school in 1961 and is now a community center.

The Hotel Prichard.
Author photo

Lodging

The Hotel Prichard, a 13-story building commissioned at a cost of $1 million by a coal baron named Frederick C. Prichard, opened at 6th Avenue and 9th Street.

The hotel was modern in every sense. It had 300 rooms, each with its own private bath, and guests could dine in a restaurant called the Hunt Club or one of 14 private dining rooms, and dance in the ballroom.

Prichard, unfortunately, lost his fortune in the Depression and had to sell the hotel. He left Huntington for Texas, but the hotel stayed open; it was converted into apartments by new owners in 1970.

Gene Autry, the singing cowboy, was one of those guests in 1949, and then-presidential candidate John F. Kennedy stayed there with his wife Jackie and brother Ted during the 1960 campaign. A hotel reception was held for the future president at 8 p.m. April 20 at the Pritchard.

Milestones

Ralph Pierre LaCock was born on March 30 in Huntington. He would go on to achieve fame under his stage name, Peter Marshall, as host of *The Hollywood Squares* TV game show.

Radio

Huntington's first radio station was also its worst radio station. It said so right there in the call letters: WSAZ reportedly stood for "Worst Station from A to Z," so christened by a radio engineer named Glenn Chase who claimed that "even a loud voice" was enough to put the station off the air.

It operated on just 50 watts of power.

Huntington's debut in the still-new medium of sound transmission didn't even start out in West Virginia. Instead, it began broadcasting in 1923 about nearly 60 miles to the north, past Point Pleasant and across the Ohio River in Pomeroy, Ohio, a tiny town of about 4,000 people.

W.C. McKellar bought the station from Chase and moved it to

Huntington in 1926, where he broadcast out of his Fourth Avenue electrical supply store. The studio was in the storefront window, and the transmitter was on the roof. Chase stayed on, working for McKellar and broadcasting the first radio program using phonograph records.

It wasn't unusual for electrical supply shops to start radio stations in the mid-1920s. Charleston Radio Supply Co. owner Walter Fredericks, a local realtor and homebuilder, had the same idea when he started WOBU a year later. Such stores wanted to sell radios, but they needed a market, so they created one by starting stations.

The Huntington Publishing Company purchased the station just a year later, in 1927, when WSAZ doubled its output to 100 watts of power and broadcast four hours a day in the evenings (except for Sundays). Each hourlong block had a different sponsor: Minter Homes, Kenny Music, and two hardware companies — Lamb & Love Electric and Hardware, and Graves-Thornton Hardware.

Sponsors paid $4 an hour for the privilege, or $24 a week.

Following the sale to Huntington Publishing, WSAZ moved its studios out of McKellar's storefront window and set up shop on the 11th floor of the Hotel Pritchard at 9th Street and 6th Avenue. (A second move, to the third floor of the Keith-Albee Theatre building, would take place in 1931.)

The station had started out at 1160 on the AM dial before moving up to 1230, and then to 1240. But that position would soon change yet again, and bring it into conflict with Fredericks' Charleston-based WOBU.

In 1928, the Federal Radio Commission decreed that WSAZ should move down to 580 on the dial, where it would share its broadcast day with WOBU. Charleston was just over 50 miles away, but their broadcast days didn't overlap, with WSAZ transmitting only in the evening, and neither's signal was powerful enough to interfere with the other's, anyway.

But that came to an end in 1930.

Times were changing, and WSAZ wanted to broadcast full time. It also had its eye on the Charleston market and wanted to boost its power output. There's no mystery why: It was simply good business sense. Charleston was almost as big as Huntington, so entering that market would double WSAZ's reach. Plus, nearly 41 percent of Charleston's population owned radio sets, compared with less than 36 in Huntington.

But Fredericks and WOBU weren't about to go down without a fight: a wavelength fight, they called it.

WSAZ wanted to eliminate the competition by purchasing WOBU, but Fredericks "point-blank refused" three overtures, even as the Huntington station appealed to the radio commission to double its power — a move that could effectively drown out WOBU's signal.

Fredericks took his case directly to Charleston residents by printing the following plea in the *Charleston Daily Mail*:

"The time is now for the citizens of Charleston to protect their own interests... With radio frequencies and facilities at a premium throughout the United States, Charleston will never again be afforded a local radio station if Huntington is permitted to arbitrarily force the capital city off the air."

Charleston's "own interests," of course, coincided with Fredericks'.

But the Huntington interests eventually won the day when the Huntington Publishing Company and WSAZ purchased the Charleston station. Instead of simply absorbing it, however, they kept the station on the air, changing the call letters to WCHS.

It turned out to be a brief marriage, though: The Huntington company sold WCHS to John Kennedy in 1936.

Then, in a stroke of irony, Kennedy took control at WSAZ, too. He acquired a stake in the station in 1939 and took over as station president, adding WSAZ to his three-station West Virginia Radio Network that included WCHS and two other stations he owned, in Clarksburg and Parkersburg.

WSAZ would operate with a Columbia Broadcasting System affiliation from 1940 to 1943 before signing on with the American Broadcasting Company in 1945.

Dreamland Pool in Kenova is seen on this vintage postcard. *Author collection*

Recreation

Dreamland Pool in Kenova really must have seemed like something out of a dream for Huntington residents during sweltering summers. When it opened, it was one of the biggest pools east of the Mississippi, at 250 feet long and half as wide.

There was actually more than one Dreamland pool: The one in West Virginia was the first, but the Dreamland Corporation opened another in Portsmouth two years later.

The Kenova pool had diving boards and a big open lawn where swimmers could "lay out," catch some rays and dry off. The attraction wasn't just for swimming, either. A three-story pavilion with a big dance floor ran the entire length of the pool, and it drew the likes of Frank Sinatra, Louis Armstrong, and Benny Goodman to perform there.

In all, the Dreamland complex covered 26 acres near the Big Sandy River.

Unfortunately, a fire destroyed the pavilion in 1972, but the pool stayed intact. The following year, the U.S. Department of Outdoor Recreation approved $225,000 to help the city of Kenova buy the pool for public use. The funds were paired with $125,000 from the Appalachian Regional Commission and $90,000 from the city.

So the pool stayed open.

A sign there in 1983 read, "You don't quit playing because you get old, you get old because you quit playing."

They were still playing at the Dreamland Pool in 2021. ...

Next door in Ceredo, there was a different kind of entertainment for the older set — the kind that many people frowned upon.

But it also drew huge crowds.

A wooden grandstand with enough room for 10,000 people was built in a former cow pasture, and the promoter, T.W. Scott of Lexington, packed 'em in. Scott was a racing promoter, and the spectators came to see — and wager on — races. Greyhound races. He spent $50,000 to build a track on land owned by the Stark family.

Henry Stark donated land next to the track for a park with picnic tables and benches.

The track opened in September with a 30-day marathon of nightly races, and the quarter-mile track became extremely popular with residents throughout the region, with additional bus and trolley service added when the events were on to accommodate overflow crowds.

All was going very well (for those who enjoyed the races, that is) until opposition to dog racing began to make things difficult for the promoters.

In May of 1927, the state Supreme Court refused to allow peri-mutuel betting on dog races — for the second time. Wayne County had shut down the races, and the promoters had sought an injunction preventing that; the court, however, refused.

Promoters made another push for racing in 1935, and the county again fought back.

An editorial in the *Hinton Daily News* sided with the county, pointing out that licenses and wagering in the state were limited by law to horse racing. "Dogs, fleas, rain drops, jumping frogs or any other subterfuge to induce people to bet are not incorporated in the law. ... Any person attempting a betting meeting other than horse-racing duly licensed by the commission is subject to a fine not less than $5,000."

The editorial continued dog racing as "a most inhumane and despicable form of gambling." It pointed to the slaughter of live rabbits during training, the near-starvation of the dogs, and the questionable character of some promoters (some of whom, it said, were controlled by mobster Al Capone).

The opponents of dog racing eventually won the day, and the meets were no longer held after 1935. From that point on, the field was used for other community events such as Ceredo-Kenova High football games, with the grandstand a convenient seating option for fans.

Unfortunately, that came to an end when a windstorm ripped off the grandstand roof in 1940, and the stands had to be demolished.

Piggly Wiggly stores no longer operate in Huntington, but they're still around. This one is in Charleston. *Author photo*

Retail

If you wanted to go grocery shopping in Huntington, you had three choices: the A&P, Kroger, or Piggly Wiggly. The A&P was the dominant chain, as it was through much of the country, with 23 locations.

Kroger had nine stores, and Piggly Wiggly had six.

A&P specialized in small corner grocers before finally following the trend toward supermarkets in the early 1940s. Some of its larger stores were in Huntington: It spend $250,000 on a new store at 1444 Madison Ave. that opened in 1946 and spent twice that much to open what was then the largest store in the entire chain at Fairfield Plaza in 1958. ...

H.L. Johnson and Jack Amsbary took over a men's haberdashery off the lobby of the Hotel Frederick.

Amsbary & Johnson later found a larger space on 10th Street, and Johnson retired, leaving Amsbary to run the place himself. He expanded the business (popularly called Amsbary's, although Johnson's name was retained even after he died) by moving it into adjacent storerooms. Then, in 1978, he moved it into the former W.T. Grant store on 3rd Avenue and 10th Street in 1978. The Grant chain had recently gone bankrupt, causing that business to close.

Amsbary remained in business until his death in 1986, and his sons carried on afterward before the store finally closed.

Transportation

Huntington finally had a way over the Ohio River, thanks to a cantilever truss bridge that carried traffic across on the new U.S. Route 52.

The new bridge connected Huntington with Chesapeake, Ohio. It was 2,594 feet long — almost half a mile — and covered with asphalt 22 feet wide. It was constructed of 7.63 million pounds of steel, held together by a million rivets.

1928

Cinema

Rae Samuels had been on stage with the Ziegfeld Follies in 1912, but on May 8, 1928, the "Blue Streak of Vaudeville" headlined the opening of the Keith-Albee Theatre. Samuels was adamant that live theater would see a resurgence, despite the increasing popularity of movie houses.

"The public wants good shows as much as it ever did," she declared a couple of years later.

The Keith-Albee Theatre in 2021. *Author photo*

"For a time, all our playwrights became scenario writers, and now they are doing talkies. What we need now is a new crop of writers, and then you just watch the public step up to the box office. ... The theater is an integral part of our life, and the personal touch with the audience can never be supplanted."

Samuels spread the gospel of live theater by touring "every town and hamlet in the U.S.A.," according to an article in the

Hinton Daily News. It was therefore ironic that she opened the theater that would be downtown Huntington's premier showcase for motion pictures.

The Keith-Albee opened at the very end of the silent film era, welcoming both live and filmed attractions. As many as 2,720 people could pack the house, including 1,200 in its balcony, to enjoy shows and music from the theater's Wurlitzer 3 organ.

The theater was part of the Keith-Albee-Orpheum chain of vaudeville and movie houses, formed early that year when Benjamin Franklin Keith and Edward Franklin Albee II combined their vaudeville group with the Orpheum theater circuit to create a chain of more than 700 U.S. movie and stage houses.

A whopping 15,000 vaudeville performers were booked through the company, which was the largest of its kind in the country.

The chain was sold to Joseph Kennedy, patriarch of the Kennedy clan that included the future president, later that year, and then to RCA, which created a new film studio called RKO (for Radio Keith Orpheum). After that, motion pictures became the primary focus, at the expense of vaudeville.

A year after it opened, the manager of the Keith-Albee was fined $10 for opening the movie house on Sundays, but the Huntington theater continued to operate through the Depression and a series of changes thereafter, retaining the Keith-Albee name throughout its history.

As many vast downtown auditoriums were, it was subdivided during the sixties to incorporate two screens in separate auditoriums, with another screen added in an adjacent space that had formerly housed retail businesses, during the seventies. It finally closed as a movie theater in 2006, but later reopened as a performing arts center.

Fairfield Stadium is shown in this Tichnor Brothers postcard. *Public domain*

Football

The Thundering Herd had a new corral: Fairfield Stadium, a 10,000-seat brick facility about a mile south of Marshall that also hosted a large number of high school games. In fact, the first game played there was between two high school teams: Huntington High and Portsmouth High from Ohio.

Huntington prevailed 18-0 in the Sept. 29 contest.

Then, in the first collegiate game played there on Oct. 7, Marshall topped Fairmont 27-0 in the second half of a double header: Huntington beat Logan High 21-0 in the first game.

The Huntington Board of Park Commissioners had purchased the site bounded by 14th and 15th streets and Charleston and Columbia avenues for $25,000 and built the stadium for $130,000. Before the facility was constructed, the site had been used as a gravel pit and garbage dump. And when it opened, park board president George Wallace joked that perhaps it should be called "Cockroach Commons."

Ultimately, the name was chosen by W.M. Prindle, who had owned the land and operated the gravel pit. He decided on

Fairfield, after his home county in Ohio.

The season proved a successful one for Marshall, which went 8-1-1 to capture the West Virginia Athletic Conference title for the second time.

1929

Community

The Cabell County War Memorial Association built a 42-foot-tall arch paying tribute to those who gave their lives during World War I.

The cornerstone was laid on Armistice Day, Nov. 11, 1924, and more than 1,000 people turned out to see the completed arch dedicated exactly five years later. The arch, made from limestone on a granite base, cost $40,000 to construct.

A plaque there lists the names of 91 men from Cabell County who died during the war, and 91 trees were planted in Memorial Park as an additional commemoration.

Memorial Arch. *Carol M. Highsmith, Library of Congress*

Flood of Troubles

1930-1939

Stewart's Original Drive-In back in its early years. *Author photo/courtesy of Stewart's*

1930

Milestones

Huntington continued to grow by leaps and bounds, adding more than 50 percent to its population total to surpass 75,000 and eclipse Wheeling as the state's largest city.

1931

Baseball

The Class-C Middle Atlantic League added a team in Huntington, the Boosters, who finished in the middle of the pack with a 68-62 record. The team would become affiliated with the Detroit Tigers for the 1932 and 1933 seasons.

1932

Stewart's Original Drive-In in 2021. *Author photo*

Fast Food

Hot dogs have always been hot commodities in Huntington, and Stewart's Original Drive-In was there at the beginning.

Stewart's root beer stands got their start in 1924 courtesy of Frank Stewart in Mansfield, Ohio, and the company began selling franchises in 1931.

That was just a year before John Louis and Gertrude Mandt built their first drive-in eatery at 2445 5th Ave. for just $1,750.

They sold two menu items at first: Stewart's Root Beer and popcorn. That's it. The hot dogs came later, with a special sauce from Gertrude Mandt's secret recipe for her homemade chili sauce.

J.L. Mandt passed away in 1942, and Gertrude retired that same year, but the stand remained in the family, with son Harry Mandt and his wife Isabelle taking the reins. Their son, another John Mandt, started working at the drive-in when he was 13 and took over in the late seventies.

His son, also named John, started working at Stewart's when he was 13, too, and later attended Marshall University. He had the idea of approaching the athletic director with the idea of making his family's hot dogs the "official" hot dogs at Marshall sporting events.

The company lost its contract with the university briefly to Marriott Corp., a private concession company that supplied its own hot dogs and even served up a sauce that was supposed to taste like Stewart's. But fans could tell the difference and started getting their hands stamped to leave at halftime and head over to Stewart's for the real thing.

Stewart's eventually won the contract back.

The family business proved so successful that the Mandts opened up other locations in Huntington: one at 1st Street and Adams Avenue, and another at 932 4th Ave., both of which have since closed.

The original location, however, remains open as of 2021, serving hot dogs with toppings that include coleslaw, bacon, jalapeños, tabasco sauce, and more standard fare such as ketchup, mustard, relish, and onions.

The menu has expanded since the early years to include burgers and sandwiches, bratwurst and corn dogs, as well as salads, wings, baked beans, cookies, veggie trays, and ice cream offerings.

Government

A citizens' committee voted George Bradshaw mayor of Huntington after his predecessor, Floyd Chapman, died in office.

Bradshaw, a local retailer and son of a prominent upstate New York physician, won by a margin of six votes in balloting on the 20-member board.

He'd been a partner in the Zenner-Bradshaw store that was consumed by fire just before Christmas in 1925 and had more recently became president of another department store in town, Bradshaw-Diehl.

1934

Baseball

The Huntington Boosters changed affiliation and changed their name to reflect the new partnership. The Boosters were now the Red Birds, farm team of the St. Louis Cardinals, for the next three seasons.

Walter Alston, future Hall of Famer and manager of the Los Angeles Dodgers, played for the Red Birds in 1936.

Walter Alston with the Brooklyn Dodgers. *Public domain*

He enjoyed perhaps his best minor-league season, hitting .326 on a career-best 157 hits with a career-high 35 home runs. One of his teammates that season was Marty Marion, who batted .268 and would go on to play 11 seasons with the St. Louis Cardinals.

1936

Dining

The French Tavern opened its doors at 2349 Adams Ave., marking the latest evolution in a business begun by Belgian immigrants George and Maria Weydisch several years back.

It had started out around 1926 as a hybrid business that combined a restaurant with a grocery service at 529 Camden Road.

After Maria passed away the following year, George remarried and, in 1932, moved the French Grocery & Meat Market to 226 Piedmont Road, where he renamed it simply the French Tavern. Belying its origins as an adjunct to a grocery store, the restaurant was a fine dining establishment that served lobster, steak, and specialties like French-style fried eggplant and French onion soup.

The restaurant stayed at that location for nearly four decades before moving up the road to a former Kroger supermarket building in 1974. By that time, it was under the ownership of Weydisch's son, George Bode, and his wife Jenni.

The new building was so big it allowed the owners to divide it into a 200-seat dining room and 190-seat supper club, along with a banquet room for as many as 250 people.

It closed six years later, in 1980.

Golf

Huntington hosted the West Virginia Open for the first time, with Sam Snead defeating Art Clark by five strokes at the Guyan Country Club. The tourney was reduced to three rounds after the second round was rained out.

It was the first of 17 victories in the tournament for Snead, who would notch his final one nearly four decades later, in 1975.

1937

Baseball

Huntington baseball ended its affiliation with the St. Louis Cardinals and reclaimed the Boosters nickname in a new league, the Class-D Mountain State League. The Boosters weren't too successful in their first season, though, going 25-58 and finishing in the league cellar.

They would change their name to the Huntington Bees the following season, after joining the Boston Bees (the nickname of the Braves at that time) as an affiliate for a season. They would revert to independent status and the Boosters name again in 1939.

They became the Aces in 1940 and '41, when they played at 5,000-seat Long Civic Field, where center field was 450 feet from home plate.

Basketball

Huntington topped Clarksburg Victory by a score of 39-28 for the state basketball crown.

Disaster

There are floods, and then there was the Great Ohio River Flood of 1937. This was in a whole different league.

There have been other floods on the Ohio River, but the scope of this one was so unprecedented that, to this day, people just call it "The Flood." No further explanation needed.

The waters began to rise on Jan. 5, and alarm bells started to sound five days later when the first flood warnings were issued. Several inches of snow had melted far more quickly than normal in a sudden stretch of warm weather punctuated by near-record rainfall even after the flood warnings started.

Looking west on 4th Avenue during the 1937 flood, with the Orpheum Theatre at left and the Hotel Frederick at right. *Public domain*

Evansville, Cincinnati, and Louisville were among the cities inundated with water: Evansville declared martial law on Jan. 23 when the water level rose to 54 feet, and nearly three-quarters of Louisville was submerged. In Cincinnati, the river rose to 80 feet, setting a record, and it rose above 60 feet in Paducah, Kentucky.

Damage was reported from Pittsburgh all the way east to

Illinois, and Huntington was not spared — not by a long shot. On Jan. 18, the river crested at just under 70 feet. That was 19 full feet above flood stage.

Local historian James Casto called the flood Huntington's version of Hurricane Katrina. The disaster left five people dead and took a toll on livestock and pets, as well. But that was just the tip of the iceberg. There were 40,000 residents living in flooded areas of town, and 25,000 of them had to leave their homes, clambering aboard C&O Railway passenger cars on special trains to higher ground in Columbus.

The passenger cars filled up quickly, so refugees settled for places on box cars or cattle cars.

Applications for aid poured in to the Red Cross: 11,000 of them. City services were offline for two weeks.

The State Theatre, left, during the 1937 flood. *Tony Rutherford, Army Corps of Engineers, Cinema Treasures, Creative Commons 2.0*

Football

Marshall, which had moved to the Buckeye Athletic Association (all the other members were in Ohio) five years earlier, won the title with a 9-0-1 record that included a 90-0 romp over Georgetown of Kentucky in a nonconference game played Oct. 22.

1938

Athletics

Cam Henderson was already coaching football and basketball at Marshall College. So what was one more sport?

Henderson took on the baseball team for a single season in 1938, compiling a 6-3 record. But his biggest successes came coaching teams on the hardwood. That shouldn't come as much of a surprise considering that Henderson was an innovator before he even got to Marshall.

When he was coaching high school ball in Bristol, West Virginia, a small community about 160 miles northeast of Huntington, he was faced with a problem: The new gym there had a leaky roof, creating slippery spots on the floor. Henderson therefore told his players to stick to specific zones on defense, creating the 2-3 zone still in use today.

He's also credited with developing the fast break. He instructed his two forwards to sprint down the sidelines after a missed basket so they could outrun the defense and score easily on a pass from the point guard.

In 1920, Henderson started coaching at the college level at Muskingum College in Ohio. After that he moved over to Davis & Elkins College in Elkins, West Virginia, where his 1924-25 basketball team went undefeated in 22 games to capture the state title. He then coached the D&E football team to a state championship in 1928; during his tenure, the school posted gridiron wins over the likes of West Virginia, Army, Navy, and Fordham.

Henderson left D&E for Marshall in 1935, having already compiled a record of 81-33-6 in football and 220-40 on the basketball court.

At Marshall, his success continued. In 20 seasons coaching basketball, he rolled up 362 wins and a winning percentage of .695. In football, he went 68-56-5 over 12 seasons.

His most successful year as a coach was undoubtedly 1947, when he led the football team to its first bowl game, the Tangerine Bowl, and coached Marshall to the NAIA championship in basketball with a record of 32-5.

But that was just the high point of a career at Marshall that was successful throughout. Henderson compiled 14 straight winning seasons as a basketball coach from 1936-37 through 1949-50, and had just one losing season in his 20 years as coach.

The Cam Henderson Center, a multipurpose athletic facility at Marshall, was named in his honor. Constructed in 1981, it seated 10,000 (though the capacity was later reduced to just over 9,000) and was the site of the world's longest recorded college basketball shot, by Bruce Morris on Feb. 7, 1985.

Dining

You might not expect to find spaghetti and steak at the same restaurant, but they've gone together just fine at Jim's Steak and Spaghetti House, which opened in 1938.

The Jim in the name was owner Jim Tweel, who started out by buying an eatery called Kennedy Dairy on June 9. He changed the name to Jim's Dairy Bar, where he served ice cream cones for a nickel, burgers for a dime, and milkshakes for 15 cents.

Later on, during World War II, the menu expanded to include

35-cent plate lunches with meat and potatoes, bread and butter, and drinks.

The spaghetti came along in 1944 when after a customer from Italy suggested it. They opened up a spaghetti house in a room they weren't using, while Tweel continued to operate the Dairy Bar separately. The two merged into a single restaurant a few years later as Jim's Grill and Spaghetti House.

Jim's Steak and Spaghetti House in 2021. *Author photo*

The name changed again in the early sixties to Jim's Steak and Spaghetti House when the restaurant took over a vacant real estate office.

Conkolene "Bunny" Gray was one of Tweel's early hires, which was significant for a couple of reasons. For one, Gray proved to be such a good worker and so valuable to the restaurant that Tweel promoted him to general manager. For another, he was Black, and although segregation wasn't as pronounced in West Virginia as it was in neighboring Virginia, it was still the rule in places like public schools when Tweel interviewed Gray for a job in 1945.

Gray had graduated from one of those segregated schools, Frederick Douglass High School, in 1942 and joined the Navy during World War II.

He applied for a job at Jim's after he was honorably discharged in 1945. He'd already worked there part-time during high school, and Tweel was happy to have him. But Gray had one condition for his hiring: that he wouldn't be hindered from moving up the ladder if he earned it.

And he did earn it. The promotion to general manager came about a decade after he was hired, which put him in charge of food preparation and also gave him a role of managing personnel, along with Tweel.

Gray wound up working at the restaurant for 60 years, finally retiring at the age of 81. He died in 2004, and Marshall University set up a memorial scholarship in his name in 2020.

Located on 5th Avenue, Jim's also features burgers, salads, fish, and sandwiches. The restaurant served up a meal for John F. Kennedy when he was running for president in 1960, and President Bill Clinton also stopped by when he was in town. Billy Joel dined at Jim's. Muhammad Ali spent a couple of hours there. Tweel's son, an attorney, represented Ali.

Today, the walls are lined with photos of all the famous people who've dined there. It's a sort of timeline that traces the history of the place, one of the iconic symbols and mainstays of downtown Huntington.

Public Works

The kind of damage caused by the flood of 1937 simply could not be allowed to happen again.

To ensure it didn't, construction began on a new Huntington Flood Wall to protect the city against future inundations. Congress had agreed to pay for the wall if the city of Huntington supplied the land. Bonds were sold to pay for acquiring the property, and a "floodwall tax" was levied on the owners of all the property the floodwall would protect.

It looks like a giant thermometer, but it's actually a gauge measuring the Ohio River water level on the flood wall built to protect the city. The river crested at just under 70 feet during the flood of 1937, which you can see is just beneath the top of the wall. *Author photo*

As with any tax, though, there were opponents.

A lawsuit was filed and went first to Cabell County Circuit Court, then to the state Supreme Court. Both upheld the bonds — and the tax — allowing the project to move forward.

The wall was built in three phases starting Aug. 1, beginning with Huntington, then Westmoreland, and finally Guyandotte. The Huntington wall was complete in 1940, and the entire wall was finished in 1943.

According to the U.S. Army Corps of Engineers' Huntington District, the wall has prevented $238.8 million in flood damage.

Track and Field

Huntington High returned to dominance in track and field, claiming the first of three consecutive state titles (although the third year was a shared championship). The team added another title in 1942.

1939

Cinema

Movie houses would soon migrate to the suburbs for good, but a few were still being built downtown in the late 1930s and into the '40s. One such theater was the Roxy, which opened at 1037 4th Ave., across the street from the Palace and down the street from the Orpheum.

It had previously operated as the Strand.

The 900-seat venue wasn't around too long in its new incarnation, though. The Roxy closed in the mid-'50s, and the building was ultimately demolished to make way for a parking garage.

Education

Huntington East High School opened at 5th Avenue and 29th Street, along with the adjacent Huntington Trades School. Auto mechanics, a program started a decade earlier at Huntington High, moved into that new facility, where courses in construction, and metal and electrical trades were also taught.

Courses would move to the new Cabell County Technology Center on Norway Avenue in 1982.

Huntington East High School. *Author photo*

Fast Food

Hot dogs, popcorn, and root beer were already a proven combination in Huntington thanks to Stewart's, and founder Strobe Fullwiller of Smith's Midway Drive-In knew a winning formula when he saw it.

When he opened in 1939, that's what he served.

Six years later, he hired Evelene Smith, who contributed the recipes for her special hot dog and barbecue sauce. One early photo of the drive-in shows an obelisk with the name MIDWAY written vertically down the center. Hires root beer was a nickel, hot dogs were 7 cents, and barbecue was 15 cents. Imperial ice cream, candy, and cigarettes were also for sale.

Smith's son, Jeff, eventually bought the restaurant, which added other menu items over the years, including hamburgers (in 1956) and milkshakes.

Ice Hockey

The Huntington Stars made their debut in the Tri-State League, a minor league that included teams in Charleston, Akron, Toledo, Youngstown, and Windsor, Ontario.

They played their home games in Arena Gardens, a steel-and-wood structure with an arched roof like a Quonset hut at 1st Street and 7th Avenue, and fared well during their three-year history. The Stars finished second behind Akron in each of their first two seasons, then won the league championship and playoff in 1941.

They went out on top, as the team folded before the start of the 1942 season, unable to put together a team with so many skaters now serving in World War II.

After the war was over, Huntington didn't field a new team. It was prevented from doing so at least in part by a spectacular fire that destroyed Arena Gardens in 1945.

Vintage street signs in the
form of an obelisk and
street tile in Huntington.
Author photos

Fires and Marshall
1940-1949

A postcard shows the interior and entrance to the Mayflower Super Dairy Store.
Public domain

1940

Bowling

Spot Lanes opened on 5th Avenue and would remain open for the next 32 years.

Dining

The Mayflower Super Dairy Store was operating around this time downtown, at the northwest corner of 4th Avenue and 11th Street.

The "store" was actually a restaurant/soda fountain, where you could sit at a booth or on one of the circular stools at the stainless steel, tile-fronted lunch counter and feast on treats like sundaes, milkshakes, and cream sodas.

Breakfast and lunch were served inside, and the entire place featured a curving Art Deco design. A cartoon cow wearing a bell and with a rather large udder greeted patrons above the front door.

Evidently, there was more than one location, because a postcard from the period refers to "stores," plural:

"The Mayflower Super Dairy Stores are located in the heart of downtown Huntington. These stores represent the very latest in architectural design and modern equipment. When in Huntington, visit the Mayflower Stores for 'Tops' in complete fountain and luncheonette service."

Milestones

The Depression had slowed population growth south of the Ohio River, just as it did in many other places, although Huntington still managed to add more than 3,000 residents, a 4.3 percent increase since 1930.

1941

Cinema

If you wanted a wide selection of movies in the 1970s, you went to a multiplex, but you could get the same thing downtown on 4th Avenue in the 1940s. There weren't any multiplexes, but there were a number of movie houses operating within easy walking distance of one another: the Palace, the Orpheum, the Keith-Albee, and the State.

The State wasn't around as long as the others, but it had its own unique reputation. It specialized in westerns and, later, was a venue for live wrestling matches.

Al Cross, who managed the theater during the Depression, said he once accepted a chicken as the price of admission in lieu of a ticket. Those were hard times.

The theater closed sometime after 1950 and was torn down to make way for an expansion of the Huntington Trust Savings Bank. ...

A 475-seat theater called the Abbott opened at 420 14th St. It would remain open until the 1980s, when it was used as a community theater. It was subsequently torn down. ...

The Beverly on Norway Avenue and Washington Boulevard was also operating by this time. The 400-seat theater closed in 1969 and became a food market two years later. ...

The Beverly on Washington Boulevard and Norway Avenue. *Elmorovivo, Cinema Treasures, Creative Commons 2.0*

1942

Baseball

With World War II underway, the Mountain State League would last just one more year, and the Huntington team was operating under yet another new name: the Jewels.

They lived up to it.

After years of struggling in the MSL, the Huntington boys found a new affiliate in the St. Louis Browns, who were two years away from winning their only American League pennant.

The Jewels ran away with the regular-season crown, soaring to an 82-42 record that was 13 games in front of their nearest rival, the Welch Miners. They had three of the league's top five players in hits — Ken Wood (who also socked 25 homers), Howard Wilson, and Edward Bachmann. And their roster also featured the circuit's two winningest pitchers in Robert Petersen (17-4) and Ribs Raney (17-7).

But none of that mattered when they got to the playoffs.

Four teams qualified, and Huntington polished off second-place Welch 2 games to 1 in the opening round.

But the fourth-place Ashland Colonels got hot at the right time. They'd barely qualified for the postseason with a 60-67 record, 23½ games behind the Jewels. They beat third-place Williamson in the semifinals, then shocked everyone by beating the Jewels 4 games to 1 for the championship.

Petersen, despite his proficiency on the mound, never played organized baseball after 1942. But Ken Wood got to the big leagues with the Browns in 1948, though he failed to duplicate his success at Huntington.

His best season in a six-year major-league career came in 1951, when he hit .237 with 15 home runs.

1943

Entertainment

Milton Supman graduated from Huntington High School with the class of '43. The name may not sound familiar to you, but his stage name just might. Soupy Sales, as he was known professionally, appeared on live television more than 5,000 times in his career, making a name for himself as a slapstick comedian.

At Huntington High, he performed at school assemblies, imitating bands, before moving on to bigger things.

Soupy Sales appears on Lunch with Soupy Sales *in 1960. Public domain*

Sales returned to Huntington after serving in the Navy during World War II and earned his bachelor's degree in journalism from Marshall College in 1949.

He worked as a reporter for $20 a week at WHTN radio in Huntington before moving to Cincinnati, where he became a deejay and adopted his stage name. It was based on a family nickname: His older brothers were known as "Ham Bone" and "Chicken Bone," so Milton became "Soup Bone." He originally called himself Milton Hines, then Soupy Hines, but changed it to Sales to avoid confusion with Heinz ketchup.

Sales later moved to television in Cincinnati, Cleveland, and Detroit's WXYZ-TV before heading out to the West Coast and settling in Los Angeles.

He became a substitute host on *The Tonight Show* and had a syndicated show called *The Soupy Sales Show* that featured two dog puppets: White Fang, the "meanest dog in the United States," and Black Tooth, the "nicest dog in the United States." He'd appear wearing a V-neck sweater, ill-fitting khaki pants, and a big polka-dotted bowtie.

He continued to do guest appearances and became one of the most recognizable faces on television.

Through it all, though, he never forgot Huntington.

When Marshall University planned its 150th anniversary celebration, some celebrity grads were charging $10,000 or $15,000 for a speaking spot.

Not Sales: He offered to appear for free.

1944

Basketball

It was a defensive battle, but Huntington High prevailed in the state finals against Woodrow Wilson by a count of 32-28, finishing the season with a record of 22-4.

Fire

A half-block of downtown stores was nothing more than smoldering rubble in the aftermath of a $500,000 blaze that tore through the two-story Miller-Ritter building on Feb. 13.

Six firefighters were injured battling the blaze, which started in a clothing store and spread quickly. Three of them were hurt when a steel safe crashed through a collapsing ceiling.

The destruction claimed four clothing stores, two shoe stores, a bakery, drugstore, sporting goods store, a financial establishment, and offices occupied by 17 tenants. The adjacent Bradshaw Diehl department store sustained $50,000 of smoke and water damage. Also damaged were a paint store and restaurant.

The fire chief, Brooks McClure, described it as the worst fire in the city's history in terms of damage.

1945

Fire

Huntington firefighters got the call shortly before midnight on April 7: Arena Gardens was burning.

They had water on the blaze five minutes after they got the call, but it was too late.

One firefighter, 52-year-old Lt. Jess Hensley, was killed and three others barely escape as the roof collapsed. Hensley's death was the first of its kind for the department. He and three other firefighters were on top of the building at the time, trying to saturate the west end of the structure.

One of them, J.P. Frazier, said he warned Hensley to be careful.

"Just then," he said, "the whole thing came out from under us. I heard the lieutenant scream, but I fell halfway through the great hole which suddenly opened up under me, and only by good luck was I able to roll to the ladder."

The two other firefighters managed to get to safety, although one suffered a broken foot jumping to the ground. Hensley's body was recovered about an hour later, untouched by the flames; he apparently died of suffocation.

Within a half-hour of their arrival, the firefighters realized it was a lost cause: The building could not be saved. They turned their attention to containing the fire so it wouldn't spread to nearby buildings.

Dick Deutsch, a local promoter who operated the Gardens, estimated the losses at $100,000 and said nothing of value was salvaged. Most of it, however, was covered by insurance. Deutsch had been the last person to leave the building at 10:15, locking the doors after the regular Saturday session of roller skating.

The cause of the fire was never discovered.

Retail

The A&P had lost its stranglehold on Huntington's grocery business by this time and was down to just two locations in the city. Piggly Wiggly and Kroger were vying for supremacy, with half a dozen stores each. ...

The Style Shop, an upscale women's store, opened in Huntington on 4th Avenue. It operated for many years in the Day & Night Building at 10th Street after its original location across 4th burned down, staying open until 1978.

1946

Dining

Karl Kirtley's Merry-Go-Round opened at 2877 5th Ave., but it wouldn't last long. Neither would its successor, Knights, which was owned by Jack Knight.

Around the time Knight's was having trouble, Ralph Wiggins was operating drive-in restaurant called the Wiggins Outside Inn at Route 60 and Washington Boulevard, behind a gas station. When Knight's became available, Wiggins opened a new business there: Wiggins Bar-B-Q.

It was across from Huntington East High School, a prime location that made it popular with students who stopped by for its milkshakes, burgers, pulled-pork sandwiches, hot dogs, strawberry pie, limeade, and the restaurant's famous spaghetti.

Wiggins sold the restaurant to a local group in 1956, and a second Wiggins restaurant opened the following year on what's now Hal Greer Boulevard (then 16th Street) at 4th Avenue, across from Marshall's Old Main building. It had previously been the site of a Pure Oil gas station and, after that, a drive-in called the Corral.

This former Pure Oil station is now an auto detailing shop. *Author photo*

Ohio-based Pure had struck a rich oil field in the Cabin Creek area near Charleston, so it had a number of Tudor-style "cottage" stations in the area. Designed by architect Carl August Peterson, they were made to look like little homes, complete with chimneys and bay windows, so they would fit in well with the neighborhood architecture.

You can still see at least a couple of them in Huntington, now converted to different uses. One at 5th Avenue and 7th Street was doing business as a car wash in 2021, while another at 8th Street and 8th Avenue had been converted into an attorney's office.

Former Pure Oil station at 8th Street and 8th Avenue. *Author photo*

As for Wiggins, the 5th Avenue location stayed open until the mid-1980s, while the one near Marshall closed in 1995. It was damaged in a fire the following year and never got rebuilt. Tascali's Decades Pasta and Grill on U.S. 60 in Barboursville acquired several Wiggins recipes, including the spaghetti, and served them until it closed in 2015. ...

The first Parkette restaurant opened at the Spring Valley Bridge in the Westmoreland neighborhood. Fred and Gloria Long opened the drive-in, the first of several in the small chain. The first stand, like many of the time, advertised a menu of root beer (for a nickel), sandwiches, and ice cream.

Six years later, the couple opened a more expansive drive-in on U.S. 60 in Kenova across from Ceredo-Kenova High School, with a large eye-catching sign advertising "fine food" and "car service" alongside a giant Porky-style cartoon pig carrying a hamburger. The pig also graced the sign on the Waverly Road Parkette, which opened two years later, and a fourth Parkette went up on 5th Avenue across from Marshall in 1960.

(The 5th Avenue Parkette eventually became a Dwight's, and the Kenova restaurant became a Fat Boy.)

Parkettes sold menu items like the Big Fred Cheeseburger Supreme for 55 cents or the Long Bill — a baked ham and cheese sandwich with pickle, lettuce, tomato, and "Long's Special Sauce" — for a nickel more. You could get egg, grilled cheese, or steak sandwiches. Or if you preferred, you could order chili, beef or pork barbecue, hot dogs, fried fish, or Italian spaghetti, the priciest item on the menu at 75 cents.

Later on, in 1977, the couple opened up Long's Family Restaurant at U.S. 60 and 6th Street in Ceredo, which they operated until 1983.

Health Care

St. Mary's Hospital completed construction of a five-story south wing. By the end of the decade, it had grown from its original 35 beds to 350.

1947

Basketball

Marshall put together a stellar season under Coach Cam Henderson, winning 17 straight games to start the season en route to a 32-5 campaign. Among the team's victims: an Indiana State team coached by none other than John Wooden, which Marshall defeated 66-58 in the season's sixth game.

Marshall qualified for the NAIB men's tournament and proceeded to start things off with a 113-80 rout of Wisconsin's River Falls State. Marshall, which set a record with its own score, won despite surrendering 56 points to Nate DeLong, a 6-foot-6 center who would go on to play a season in the NBA.

But things got more difficult from there. Two of the next three games were decided by a single point, as Marshall edged Hamline of Minnesota 55-54 in the second round, with Andy Tonkovich scoring three points in the last minute of play, before topping Eastern Washington 56-48 to make the semifinals.

There, Cam Henderson's team ran into Emporia State of Kansas, which bolted out to a lead before the Thundering Herd came thundering back and tied it in regulation, then eked out a 56-55 win in overtime before a tournament-record crowd of 8,000.

The finals pitted offensive-minded Marshall against the Minnesota State Teachers College of Mankato, a defensive powerhouse that had beaten Arizona State 52-46 in the other semifinal.

Marshall ran out to an early lead against Mankato, but the Minnesotans closed the gap to 32-30 at halftime and tied the score early in the second half. Marshall reclaimed the lead, but was still only four points ahead with 5 minutes to play.

That's when Marshall's Jim Bakalis went to work, scoring 12 points off the bench to help the Herd pull away and claim the title. Bill Hall, who had eight field goals in the first half, finished with 27 points to lead the scoring.

Hall, Tonkovich, and Gene James were all named first-team NAIB All-Americans, and Bill Toothman was a second-team choice.

The conquering heroes returned to a greeting of 15,000 jubilant fans in Huntington.

They'd be back in the NAIB tourney the following season after winning the Los Angeles Invitational. (They beat Syracuse 46-44 for the title.) In the postseason, the Herd won their first-round NAIB game 72-53 over Peru State of Nebraska, but then fell in double-overtime, 74-72, to San Jose State in the second round. ...

Huntington East wrapped up a 22-4 season by beating South Charleston 47-44 to capture the Highlanders' first state title. They would return to the finals the following year, despite a more modest 16-11 record, but were no match for heavily favored Princeton, which concluded a 25-1 campaign with a 48-35 win.

Fast Food

World War II veteran Paul Ward Sr. opened Wards Do-Nuts on 4th Avenue at 14th Street, a 24-hour business serving "deliciously different do-nuts" made from an old Tennessee family recipe, alongside Coca-Cola products and Sealtest ice cream. It was a gathering spot for college students and a popular late-night hangout for everyone from cab drivers to university students cramming for exams.

Ward later opened a second location at 4th Avenue and 1st Street that served chili that rivaled his donuts in popularity. But the donuts were always the main attraction.

Ward made them with mashed potatoes or potato starch so they were extra fluffy, and he lit up the store's round sign in the middle with the word "HOT" whenever a new batch was ready for sale.

If any of that makes you think of Krispy Kreme donuts, here's another interesting piece of trivia: Ward originally incorporated the words "Crispy Creme" in name of his shop, but he had to scrub the words off the front of the building when Krispy Kreme threatened to sue him. You could still see the faded lettering on the brickwork, though.

The original Ward's stayed open until 2000, when Ward sold his equipment and closed up shop, selling the building to Rocco Muriale of Rocco's Ristorante, who transformed it into Rocco's Little Italy.

Football

Marshall posted a 9-2 record and qualified for a trip south to Orlando, where the team played in its first bowl game, the Tangerine Bowl on Jan. 1, 1948.

Marshall hadn't had many problems putting points on the board that season, scoring 30 or more seven times, but came up empty against a stubborn Catawba defense that entered the game with nine shutout wins and just one loss.

The two teams battled to a scoreless tie for the first 55½ minutes before Catawba fullback Lee Spears found the end zone from a yard out to cap a 45-yard drive in which he carried the ball on 10 of 12 plays.

Marshall tried to counter, going 66 yards after the ensuing kickoff before the drive stalled at the Catawba 26. Catawba then ran out the clock.

Despite the loss, the Herd dominated the game statistically, rolling up 109 yards on the ground to just 54 for their opponents, and making 12 first downs, twice as many as Catawba.

1948

Cinema

Most drive-in theaters went up on the outskirts of big cities, and the Ceredo Drive-In was no exception. The first drive-in to go up in the Huntington area, it had room for 300 cars. It opened June 4 on the western side of land that had once been home to the community's popular greyhound track in the late twenties and early thirties.

(On the eastern side, 25 acres were devoted to the Wayside Golf Course.)

1949

Baseball

Huntington East defeated Moorefield 5-3 for the West Virginia state championship.

Sam Snead hits a shot at the 1934 New South Wales tournament. *Ted Hood, public domain*

Golf

Sam Snead made history at the Spring Valley Country Club in Huntington, winning his fifth West Virginia Open with a 17-under-par showing.

And it wasn't even close.

Snead shot a 65 and 68 over the final two rounds to finish

with a four-round total of 263 on the par-72 course. Runner-up George Hoffer of Wheeling finished a distant second, 18 shots off the pace after fading with a 78 in the final round.

Snead's four-round total matched the record for the 5,600-yard layout at Spring Valley.

"Slammin' Sammy" had close ties to West Virginia. In fact, he became the resident pro at Greenbrier Resort in White Sulphur Springs in 1944.

Snead had won the West Virginia Open in Huntington before, back in 1936 when he beat Art Clark by five strokes at the Guyan Country Club. He was also the defending tournament champion, having won at the Wheeling Country Club a year earlier, where Hoffer had been the runner-up as well.

Mack & Dave's was closed by 2021. *Author photo*

Retail

Mack & Dave's had it all. The business opened in 1949 and moved to a block-long space on 3rd Avenue a quarter century later. Mack Webb and David Cohen got things going by purchasing the pawn shop where they were both employed, B&B Loans.

The store sold a line of products that included furniture, electronics, jewelry, musical instruments, cameras, and guns. ...

Tradewell, a locally based grocer, had opened at 911 8th St. to break the Kroger-Piggly Wiggly stranglehold on Huntington. The company would open other locations in town and would remain in business until the early 1990s.

Television

WSAZ had been a radio station for the more than two decades. Now, it was something else, too — something very different.

It was a television station.

WSAZ-TV began broadcasting in 1949. *Author photo*

The Huntington Publishing Company was expanding its horizons and sending out a new kind of signal: one that could be picked up by that still relatively rare breed of transmission receiver called the TV set.

The first regular program, *Stop the Music*, was telecast in late October, but the first broadcast days were far from 24 hours. Those were the years of test patterns after the late news. And in fact, WSAZ was on the air just 10 hours in September of 1950, starting at 1 p.m. Scheduled programming included *Kukla, Fran, and Ollie*; *Sports Almanac*; *Kraft Theater*; and *Break the Bank*.

Barely a month after the first telecast, WSAZ was at Fairfield Stadium in Huntington for the Thanksgiving Day football game between Marshall and Xavier. Xavier won 13-7, but it didn't diminish the significance of such an early live sports broadcast.

Huntington at its Peak

1950–1959

Veterans Memorial Fieldhouse opened in 1950 and was the home to Marshall basketball, as well as the venue for a variety of other events, for decades. *Public domain photos*

1950

Athletics

Marshall College's basketball team broke in the new Memorial Fieldhouse with a resounding 84-34 victory over Fairmont State.

Bob Koontz scored 24 points, and Don Brown added 20 in the blowout.

The arena, which seated 6,500 people for basketball, hosted Marshall basketball games and also was home to high school state championship games, rotating with Charleston and Morgantown from 1962 to 1970.

State Catholic championship games were also held there from 1950 to 1979.

Cinema

The East Outdoor Theatre had just one screen, but there was room for 1,077 cars.

June Haver starred in the opening feature, *I'll Get By*, and the theater offered added opening-night incentives to boost its turnout: rides for the kids and fireworks.

The theater was open nightly "rain or shine," and offered free baby bottle warming. There was also a miniature golf course and what was described as "a unique swimming and fishing pool." By the 1960s, it was so popular that it was filled to capacity on weekends and sometimes even on weeknights.

Drive-ins had been using ramps to help car occupants get a good view of the screen since the system was patented in 1932. But the East employed a double-ramp system to accommodate more patrons. (In such a system, because the ramps are closer together and at different heights, more cars can fit in the same space.)

The East was the biggest drive-in in the area. *Elmorovivo and William, Cinema Treasures Creative Commons 2.0*

Junior Ross, longtime manager of the East, said in a 1992 newspaper article that he could recall a time when "popcorn was sold before it was popped and every spot on the gravel lot was filled."

If you were low on gas, you could fill up at an Exxon station right next door, and if you wanted a meal before or after the show, you could stop by a Shoney's that hugged right up against the outer fence of the drive-in.

Thanks to that popularity, the East survived longer than many other drive-ins, but it closed for good in 1993.

East theater owner Dick Hyman explained it in practical terms at the time: "We face the same problems as many drive-in theaters. The land underneath is more valuable than what it's being used for."

Fast Food

The Messinger family opened the Adkins Fat Boy Drive-In, named Dwight Messinger's father, Benny Adkins. It was the first of eight such establishments opened over the next four years: four of them in Huntington, and two each in Parkersburg and Chesapeake, Ohio.

Messenger used his own name in opening up Dwight's Drive-In at 8th Street and 9th Avenue in 1963.

Dwight's offered some variations on the standard fare, including the Brawny Lad, a burger on a rye bun with onions and tomatoes; fish sandwiches; and its Husky Steak Sandwich (9-inch beef steak on a fried bun), which was served with hand-breaded onion rings.

McDonald's may have had the Big Mac, but Dwight's had a double-beef-patty feast it dubbed the Kingburger.

In '71, a second Dwight's location — this one open 24 hours — replaced and Adkins Fat Boy at 601 1st St. The Messinger family also opened a full restaurant called the Steak n' Kettle, and both Dwight's locations remained open for some time.

The original closed in 1995, and the 1st Street location shut its doors eight years later, but a St. Albans location that opened in 1993 remained open as of 2020.

It was still offering the classic menu and was still run by the Messinger family.

The Tipton Theater featured a huge tower sign out front. *Granola, Cinema Treasures, Creative Commons 2.0*

Fire

The Tipton Theater had opened just three years earlier, a majestic movie house with an 80-foot tower above the marquee and 1,000 seats inside.

When a fire that spread from the J.C. Penney building got through with it, the theater was a total loss.

It was never rebuilt.

The fire started with a gas explosion in Penney's basement furnace room, then crossed an alley to engulf the theater. News reports described how transformers in the alley between the department store and the theater "exploded from the heat, causing the high-voltage lines to break and crackle in the street."

A taxi driver called just before 5 a.m. to report the blaze, but it took firefighters three hours to bring it under control.

By the time they did, both the theater and the store were gutted. Penney's lost an estimated $400,000 worth of stock, but damage at the theater was even worse. The façade and lobby appeared untouched, but the auditorium was a jumble of twisted steel girders, rafters, ruined seats, and ash.

Other businesses were badly damaged by smoke and water: Silver's 5 and 10 Cent Store, Gold Furniture, Monarch Café, and Neubert Shoes.

Damage from the fire was estimated at upwards of $1.5 million.

The fire came just weeks after a $200,000 blaze destroyed the West Virginia Electric Co. building across the street from J.C. Penney, which, amazingly, was able to restore its interior and eventually reopen after the fire.

Milestones

Huntington reached its population peak with the help of the postwar baby boom, topping 86,000 residents with a 9.5 percent growth rate during the 1940s. But the population would enter a decline in the '50s that continued into the next millennium.

1952

Health Care

Voters approved a $3 million bond for a new hospital on an overwhelming vote, casting 88 percent of their ballots in favor of the project.

Transportation

The Tri-State Airport was dedicated three miles south of Huntington.

Piedmont Airlines was the first company to provide air service to and from the airport, via DC-3s in 1952, with Eastern and Allegheny arriving the following year. Piedmont's 737s were the first jets to use the airport, starting in 1969.

Piedmont and Allegheny would eventually join forces to form USAir (later US Airways), which merged with American Airlines in 2015.

1953

Lodging

The Stone Lodge Motel was "new in 1953," according to a postcard.

Seven miles east of downtown on U.S. 60 and 10 East, the motel operated by Mr. and Mrs. Pau Taylor offered "every accommodation of the VERY BEST," with amenities including furnace circulating heat, air conditioning, foam rubber beds, oak furnishings, and ceramic tile baths.

Single and family units were available.

A later postcard, from the 1960s, showed that the motel had become a member of Quality Courts, the forerunner of Quality Inns, and was approved by AAA. Following an expansion, it had 72 units with TVs, radios, and phones, and guests could take advantage of a "good dining room," swimming pool, and playgrounds.

The managers were now Mr. and Mrs. Howard King.

Still later, the motel became affiliated with Best Western.

It had a nightclub, called the Mill Run, that was popular during the 1970s, and Ming's restaurant — famous for Ming Eng's cinnamon rolls — relocated from the old Hotel Frederick downtown to the Stone Lodge in 1998 before closing in 2009.

Transportation

Charleston architect George D. Brown designed a new bus station for Greyhound, which was built at 1251 4th Ave. in the Streamline Moderne style that was then popular.

Previously, Greyhound had operated out of the former Baltimore & Ohio Railroad station.

The Huntington Greyhound Station.
Author photo

1954

Basketball

Hal Greer was recruited by coach Cam Henderson to play basketball at Marshall, becoming the first Black athlete (or even student) to attend a "white" college in West Virginia.

Greer had been a guard for the Douglass High School team in

Huntington, where he had averaged more than 15 points a game and been named to the all-state and all-regional teams as a senior.

He did even better during his first year at Marshall, averaging 17 points a game for the college's freshman team, and went on to average 19.4 for his career at the school — including 23.6 points as a senior.

Hal Greer went on to a long NBA career and had a street named after him in Huntington. *Author photo, above, and public domain*

Greer would go on to have a sensational run in the National Basketball Association. Joining the Syracuse Nationals in 1958, he played his entire career with the same franchise, moving with the team to Philadelphia in 1964 when it became the 76ers.

Greer made 10 consecutive all-star teams starting in 1960-61, when he averaged 19.6 points a game. He averaged 20 points or more eight times, including for seven straight seasons, posting a career-high 24.1 in 1966-67 and playing alongside Wilt Chamberlain on the 1968 NBA championship team.

When he retired after 15 seasons, Greer was one of just five players to have played that long.

Huntington honored him by renaming 16th Street (State Route 10) as Hall Greer Boulevard in 1978, and he was elected to the Naismith Basketball Hall of Fame in 1982.

Dining

Alex Schoenbaum opened his first Shoney's restaurant in Huntington, and that was a problem — because it wasn't called Shoney's at the time. It was called the Parkette Big Boy, which created some confusion, considering Long's Parkette already had two locations in Huntington at the time.

It wasn't long before Schoenbaum's enterprise had a new name. More on that in a bit.

Schoenbaum's restaurant at 2501 5th Ave. and 25th Street was the first of two he opened on 5th over the next couple of years. They marked the debut of Schoenbaum's business in Huntington, but he wasn't new to town.

In fact, Schoenbaum had moved with his family to Huntington when he was 10 years old. His father owned the Arcade Recreation bowling alley and pool room there, and the younger Schoenbaum worked as a pin boy in the establishment, resetting the pins after each ball thrown — this was before the days of automated pinsetters.

After high school, he went off to college and became a standout tackle for Ohio State on the gridiron, twice earning honorable mention All-American status and being picked 55th overall in the NFL Draft by the Brooklyn Dodgers football team. When he returned, though, he didn't go back to Huntington, but to Charleston. His family had a bowling alley there, too, and he became the manager.

In 1947, he opened a restaurant next to the bowling alley, which he dubbed the Parkette Drive-In — not to be confused with Long's Parkette restaurants in Huntington.

A 1951 wintertime ad in the *Charleston Daily Mail* proclaimed you didn't "have to be an Eskimo to enjoy the good food at the Parkette. For in all kinds of weather, you still get the same courteous service that go to make the Parkette one of Charleston's finest eating places."

The Parkette "on the Boulevard" served a selection of dishes including burgers, hot dogs, chili, barbecue sandwiches, chicken, and seafood.

In 1952, Parkette became the Big Boy licensee for West Virginia and expanded from there: An ad in the February *Daily Mail* bragged, "You can now get a Big Boy at the Parkette. Don't miss this sensational treat!" (The affiliation, which began in 1952, would end about three decades later.) Big Boy had started out at Bob's on the West Coast, and Schoenbaum became the biggest licensee in the eastern United States.

Whether spurred by a desire to avoid confusion with Long's Parkette or simply because he wanted a catchier name, Schoenbaum launched a renaming contest in 1954, asking for suggestions from the public. No purchase was necessary — not even a Big Boy — and the prize was a 1954 Lincoln hardtop convertible.

The winning suggestion was Shoney's, and the chain became known by that name in 1954. An insurance rep from Charleston named Paul S. Edens won the car... and promptly sold it.

The first two Huntington restaurants were both on 5th Avenue: at 25th Street — later 21st Street — and 10th Street. More restaurants came later, on Washington Avenue in 1979, and out by the East Drive-In. At its peak in 1998, Shoney's would have more than 1,300 chain and franchise restaurants in 34 states.

There was even a motel chain that operated for some years beginning in 1975 called Shoney's Inn.

The chain would be immortalized in a song by country music artist Joe Diffie called "Third Rock from the Sun," in which a truck "hits a Big Boy in the Shoney's parking lot," triggering a chain of events in which the Big Boy statue hits a bank clock, which in turn strikes a light pole that causes a power outage all over the city.

And rumors that a giant alien had landed at the mall.

No word on whether any of this fictional account was supposed to have occurred in Huntington.

SHONEY'S

Lodging

The Gateway Motel provided a gateway to both the past and future in Huntington.

Located eight miles east of the city center on U.S. 60, it was right off the highway and provided travelers with a convenient alternative to downtown hotels. That part wasn't exactly new. Motels, or motor courts as they were more commonly known until the fifties, had been a growing trend since the federal highway system was introduced in 1926.

Some motels, like the Tourist Motel at 343 Washington Ave., operated right in "the heart of Huntington." It housed modern facilities inside sturdy (and fireproof) stone construction, with tile baths, air-cooled rooms, central heat, comfortable furnishings, and jalousie windows and doors for maximum privacy.

The Tourist Motel offered "a comfortable night's rest for the legitimate tourist and commercial traveler," warning off supposedly illegitimate riffraff.

But most motels were outside the city limits, where they didn't have to compete with luxury hotels and could offer their own advantages, such as free parking and less traffic. Many of them in the Huntington area were on Route 60.

The 4 in One Modern Motel, owned by a certain J. Marcum, was open in the mid-1950s on Route 60 two miles east of the city limits, providing its guests with steam heat in the winter and A/C in the summer, inner spring mattresses, hot and cold running water, and private toilets and baths.

The Gateway, when it opened, didn't seem much different than other motels of the day. It had 18 units at first, and added four more within its first two years, advertising air conditioning, steam heat, telephones, and free in-room television: "Southern Hospitality with Modern Comfort." It was AAA-approved and "recommended by Duncan Hines."

By the mid-sixties, however, the motel looked much different. An ambitious expansion project added a new wing with 250 rooms, making it the largest motel in the region. It had a popular restaurant, and a conference center was added in the 1980s, when it changed its name to the Gateway Inn and Conference Center.

The owners operated the business as a Holiday Inn for a while and made $200,000 in additional investments before switching over to Best Western in 1997. The upgrades weren't enough to save the aging inn, though, and the owners filed for bankruptcy four years later, selling off all the hotel's furnishings and other items and closing their doors for good.

Recreation

In 1954, backyard swimming pools were still a rarity. Cooling off and getting into the swim of things was something you had to travel to do, and if you weren't close to a beach or a lake, you needed a pool.

Now, at long last, Huntington had one.

Sure, you could go to Dreamland in Kenova or across the river to the new Riverside Club in Chesapeake, which had a 105-by-200-

foot pool, along with other recreational activities like tennis, roller skating, and badminton. But it was a members-only operation, and yearly dues were required.

Huntington's new Olympic Pool, on the other hand, wasn't. But it didn't happen overnight, or even over the course of just one year. The city kept trying to build it, and one thing or another seemed to get in the way. It wasn't until the Women's Interclub Council got involved that the project got off the ground — and, eventually, *in* the ground.

The club proposed a tax that would fund construction of the big Olympic Pool at 12th Street West and Memorial Boulevard along with others in the community over three years at a cost of $400,000. The idea worked.

On Memorial Day 1954, all the new pools opened, just in time to welcome the summer season. The Olympic Pool had two slides and a "sprinkling mushroom," along with concession stands. It remained a popular hotspot (or cool spot) for youths until the 1990s, when attendance began to drop off and the pool found itself in need of repair.

The pool closed after the summer of 2000 and remained closed until volunteers succeeded in reopening it four years later. By 2006, however, the pool was not only closed again but torn down altogether.

Still, it outlasted the Riverside Club, which closed in the late seventies.

1956

Basketball

Marshall won its only Mid-American Conference men's basketball title, with Hal Greer setting a school record by shooting 60 percent from the field and averaging 15.5 points a game.

The team finished 18-5 in its first season under new coach Jule Rivkin, as senior center Charlie Slack led the way at 22.6 points and 23.6 rebounds a game.

Football

Quarterback Howard Bennett from Beckley, West Virginia, and halfback Roy Goines, from Huntington's all-Black Douglass High School broke the color barrier at Marshall. The pair became the first two African-American varsity football players for the college.

Health Care

The new Cabell Huntington Hospital opened its doors to patients, providing 236 beds initially and increasing that to 280 in 1963.

A second expansion in 1976 would add 30 more beds as well as E.R. and radiology facilities, a cafeteria, and business offices. Expansions of the surgery suite, recovery room, and physical therapy department were also part of this Phase II expansion.

Ice Hockey

"Hockey Back In Huntington After 15 Year Absence," proclaimed a headline in the Beckley Post-Herald.

Unfortunately, it didn't stay long, but it was fun while it lasted.

Huntington hadn't had a team since the Stars won the title during their third and final season in the Tri-State League, but now they had a team in a more prestigious circuit: the International Hockey League.

The Grand Rapids Rockets had relocated from Michigan and would play their games in the 4,100-seat Veterans Memorial Fieldhouse, built in 1950 on 5th Avenue. The team was partly owned by Ernie Berg, who also owned another team in the league, the Fort Wayne Komets.

Rounding out the circuit that year were Indianapolis, Cincinnati, Troy (Ohio), and Toledo.

The community was introduced to the new Huntington Hornets with a parade and a free instructional clinic in October.

Fort Wayne was the opening opponent in a 60-game schedule.

The team had two players who had, or would have, NHL experience: Defenseman Bob Wilson had played one game with the Chicago Blackhawks three seasons earlier, while left wing Len Ronson would see action in 13 games with the New York Rangers in 1960-61 and in five games with the Oakland Seals in 1968-69. Neither, however, was the Hornets' biggest star.

Center Ronnie Spong from Toronto led the Hornets in both goals with 25 and points with 54, while Don Davidson's 30 assists were tops in that category.

The Hornets finished third in the standings with a record of 26-30-4 and advanced to the playoffs, but attendance wasn't what Berg had hoped it would be, so he started seeking a new home for the team before the season was too far along.

Dick Deutsch, who had been involved in promoting Arena Gardens when the Stars played there, tried to buy the team, but he and other investors couldn't put together the $30,000 Berg was asking. An offer of $9,000 was followed by another of $15,000, and Berg countered by coming down from his original figure to $22,000.

But that still wasn't low enough, and he wound up selling to a group from Louisville instead, where the team became the Louisville Rebels the following season.

1957

The Elks Lodge building on 4th Street. *Author photo*

Community

The Elks Lodge building on 4th Street got a $250,000 facelift as the lodge's membership reached its peak at about 2,000.

The building was originally constructed in 1909 at a cost of $50,000 and opened on New Year's Day 1910 with a dance attended by 1,000 people and a cannon salute.

The building included a public restaurant in the basement, a reading room and offices on the ground floor, the lodge meeting room on the second floor, and a third-story ballroom.

Dining

Campbell Hagge opened Cam's Ham at 8th Avenue and 1st Street, selling a selection of items like hot dogs, sandwiches, and beer. It was more like a grocery store than a restaurant, but that didn't last.

He moved to a different building next door two years later and eventually dispensed with selling groceries to focus on dining in. The focal point of the business quickly became Hagge's Sugar Flaked Ham Sandwich, served on a toasted bun with lettuce and a sweet sauce Hagge concocted himself.

Other items on the menu included a two-patty burger called the Big Beefer, and roast beef and barbecue beef sandwiches, and battered onion rings.

Milestones

Michael W. Smith was born Oct. 7 in Kenova. He would go on to achieve success as a contemporary Christian recording artist, best known for his 1991 crossover hit "Place in This World," which reached No. 6 on the Billboard Hot 100.

Retail

Those crazy news sounds called rock 'n' roll were spinning off local record players and flying out the doors of Davidson's Record Shop at 907 4th Ave.

Young people flocked to Davidson's after school to find the latest discs from Elvis, the Big Bopper, Buddy Holly, Jerry Lee Lewis, and their other favorites. The store was so packed there was little elbow room to spare.

When Davidson's opened in 1957, it was the first store of its kind. Until then, if you wanted to find the latest 45s, you'd have to go to a department store or music store. Davidson's was the first outlet in West Virginia to deal solely in records.

It wasn't the last, though.

National Record Mart opened later on, next to Nick's News and across from the courthouse. The chain had begun in

Pittsburgh in 1937 as Jitterbug Records and, at its peak, had more than 130 locations. There was also Audio Tapes and Records, and Dr. Feel Good's Record Emporium was open in Barboursville by the 1970s.

Gary Fizer opened Sights 'n Sounds, where you could find hard rock albums and, later on, CDs.

1958

Health Care

The original St. Mary's hospital buildings were both history. A new convent was being built to replace the old converted gymnasium, and would be complete by 1959. The old prep school was torn down, too, and a new six-story east wing was built in its place.

Retail

Sears left its downtown store at 823 4th Ave., where it had operated since the 1920s, and moved to a new standalone location with room for free parking that wasn't available downtown.

The new store was at 5th Avenue and 29th Street. Sears would remain at that location until it moved into the Huntington Mall as a founding anchor tenant in 1981.

1959

Bowling

Bowling was all the rage, as leagues were forming across the country. Automated pinsetters, introduced earlier in the decade, made it easy to play with minimum wait times, and an argument could be made that bowling, not baseball, had become the national pastime.

It was in this environment that a pair of Huntington businessmen, Jack Hyman and Lloyd Frankel, teamed up to build Colonial Lanes. Ground was broken at 626 Fifth St. West on the $750,000, 24-lane bowling center in September, and it opened ahead of schedule around Christmas.

Strike Zone Bowling Center off U.S. 60. *Author photo*

There was parking for 130 cars in the lot, a nursery for the kids, underground ball returns, and automatic pin-spotters. (Strike Zone, another bowling center, would open the following year and was still operating in 2021.)

But Colonial Lanes earned a reputation as much for its food as its bowling. You don't usually think of a bowling alley as a destination for fine dining, but in this case, it was, thanks to Frankel's Rebels and Redcoats Tavern.

It didn't start out that way.

When it first opened, the eatery was called the Taproom and served standard bowling bar fare like beer on tap and corned beef sandwiches with cream cheese and onions. It was added as part of an expansion that included 10 new lanes on top of the original two dozen. But in 1967, Frankel remodeled it in partnership with Charlie Neighborgall to create Rebels and Redcoats, a full restaurant that offered the likes of prime rib and lobster bisque, along with a complete wine list.

Food came to your table on pewter plates, and wine was served in red glass goblets.

That wine service was made possible by a new 1961 law in Virginia that allowed restaurants and bars to sell liquor by the drink to anyone with a nominal "membership" at the establishment. That could involve nothing more than paying an extra dollar to become a "member" when you bought your first drink, and allowed restaurants all over the state to start serving alcoholic beverages.

Frankel and Neighborgall totally remodeled the old Taproom. A large fireplace served as a centerpiece for the Colonial-style room, where live music was played. Two years after it opened, in 1969, it earned four-star status, and later became the city's only five-star restaurant.

In 1976, the *Sunday Gazette-Mail* of Charleston published a piece by Delmer Robinson, who picked out the best restaurants in different cities around the state.

"In Huntington, it's no question," he wrote. "It's Lloyd Frankel's 'Rebels and Redcoats' at 626 Fifth St. W., adjoining Colonial Lanes. It's a labor of love for Frankel, who recently was named 'restaurateur of the year' for his contributions to the industry, but also deserves the honor for his contributions to the well-being and pleasure of his patrons. Rebels and Redcoats serves nothing but prime meat, and a rack of lamb I had there recently was a delight."

The restaurant stayed open until 2004, when it scaled back

and became just a tavern again. The bowling alley itself closed in 2018 after nearly six decades in business.

Cinema

If you wanted to see a drive-in movie, you could visit the East or the Ceredo. But in 1959, you had another option, too. You could go across the river and visit the Tri-State Drive-In in Chesapeake, Ohio.

The Tri-State, built for $190,000, had the biggest screen in the area. It opened up on June on County Road 1 with a capacity of 800 vehicles and a box office built especially for the car-bound customer: The floor was a foot and a half below ground, so the ticket-taker was at eye-level with the driver.

The Tri-State showed its last movie Sept. 8, 1981.

There were other options, too.

The Super 52 Drive-In was open on U.S. 52, as listed in the January 1966 edition of *Box Office*. Also up Route 52 in Burlington was the Burlington Auto Theater, five minutes from Huntington, which was charged 75 cents a person in 1963 and proclaimed itself "your family theater."

In 1958, patrons there were treated to a harrowing but somewhat comical sight when a fire broke out amid a film showcasing sharks and skin divers. Water was being shown on the screen, and soon there was *real* water on the screen as well.

The volunteer firemen who arrived to fight the blaze sprayed water onto the screen, but the show went on. Faulty wiring was blamed, and the damage was limited to $250.

Community

Fairfield Stadium was the site of "Caballrama," a festival marking the 150th anniversary of Cabell County that featured 1,500 singers, dancers, and actors.

The Frostop Drive-In is known for its giant root beer mug, which still rotates on top of the roof. *Author photos*

Fast Food

Yes, that's a giant root beer mug on top of that building, but no, you can't drink out of it. The mug atop the drive-in restaurant at 1449 Hal Greer Blvd. is a signature piece for what was once an expansive chain that peaked at 350-plus outlets around 1960.

Most of them were in the Midwest and Deep South (where po' boy sandwiches were popular menu items), but locations could be found as far afield as Florida, New York, California, and Washington state.

By 2021, though, there were just 13 left, nearly half of them in Louisiana.

One, however, was still operating in Huntington.

It had been there since 1959, when Rupert McGinnis and Bill Murdock opened up to customers for the first time. And it was still a family business 60 years later, run by Marilyn McGinnis Murdock (Rupert McGinnis' daughter and Bill Murdock's niece). Larry Turner, the store manager, had been for 35 of those first 60 years.

The Frostop chain started with a root beer stand in Springfield, Ohio, back in 1926, just five years after the nation's first drive-in opened. The first big mug appeared atop the roof of the building in Jefferson, Louisiana, in 1954, and the drive-in today serves a selection of items that included hot dogs, burgers, sandwiches (chicken, pork, and ham), fries, and shakes. Many Frostops make their own root beer right on the premises.

The Frostop franchise went out of business in the 1980s, but there's a company that makes the root beer and crème sodas, which are still sold in stores such as Rural King and Ace Hardware.

Retail

A Big Bear arrived in town... and started selling groceries.

The chain had been in business since the early 1930s in Ohio, but this was its first location in Huntington, in the Fairfield Plaza shopping center on 16th Street (now Hal Greer Boulevard).

Former heavyweight champ Rocky Marciano and a group of performing bears appeared at the grand opening.

There were about to be a lot more choices when it came to

grocery shopping in town. By 1965, Tradewell had six locations in the area, Evans had four, Freshway had three, and there was a Tower Grocery out on U.S. 60 in Barboursville.

Piggly Wiggly had vanished from the scene in the 1950s, while A&P still had three stores, and Kroger was down to two.

But Big Bear kept on getting bigger.

It opened a second store in 1962 at 115 6th Ave., where Huntington Memorial Hospital used to be, and added another in 1976 at the Ceredo Plaza Shopping Center.

The Big Bear chain was sold in 1989 to a Syracuse company, which went out of business 15 years later, taking the remaining Big Bear stores with it. The first Huntington Big Bear and the other stores at Fairfield Plaza were ultimately torn down to make room for the Cabell Huntington Hospital parking lot.

Civil Rights and Blue Laws

1960–1969

1960

Golf

The West Virginia Open was back at the Spring Valley Country Club, and the result was the same as it had been 11 years earlier — although it was a lot closer this time.

Sam Snead won it again. For the ninth time.

But he was so convinced he wouldn't come out on top that he packed up and left an hour and a half before the issue was decided, having just

Sam Snead in 1967. *Public domain*

posted a 3-under-par 67 for the final round.

"I was lousy," Snead lamented after he finished play. "I lost interest after the ninth hole," which he bogeyed.

Art Wall and Arnold Palmer were still on the course when Snead departed, and Wall seemed in good position to overtake him. But even though he was just a stroke off the pace with eight holes to play, he didn't manage a single birdie down the stretch, and Snead's one-stroke margin held up.

Unfortunately for Snead, he wasn't around to pick up the $1,200 winner's check, which state Gov. Cecil Underwood had flown in by helicopter to deliver. But it wouldn't be his last victory at the event: Snead would win the tournament a total of eight more times. His last victory came in 1975 (his fourth in a row), at the age of 63.

Milestones

Huntington's population dipped slightly (3.2 percent) to 83,627, as Charleston briefly surpassed it as the largest city in the state. The two cities would duel for the top spot on the population chart for the rest of the century.

1961

Baseball

Huntington downed Woodrow Wilson 5-2 in the state baseball finals, the first of three state titles in a six-year span. The Pony Express topped Romney 6-1 in 1964 and Wellsburg 5-1 two years later.

Competition

A 19-year-old Marshall University freshman named Jo Ann Odum won the Miss World-USA title at Carnegie Hall. She would go on to finish seventh in the Miss World global competition.

Odum won the crown over 18-year-old Janet Marie Boring of Long Island, and became the first beauty pageant winner ever invited to the White House.

Unlike some other pageant winners, Odum never sought the spotlight afterward.

When asked after winning what she'd like to be doing 10 years later, she answered that she hoped to be the mother of two or three children. And that's exactly what she became. She married an insurance agent, moved to Delaware, had a couple of sons, and volunteered teaching Bible classes and charm school at a women's prison.

"I enjoyed every moment of my pageant experience," she would say in a 1978 interview. "I was in 14, and even losing a couple of them helped me grow up — and I never felt 'used.' From there, I chose the quiet life. I wanted to marry, and do it well, with no career interference. I was never attracted to the life of an entertainer."

Basketball

Favored Huntington High lived up to its billing with a 78-71 triumph over Woodrow Wilson in the state championship game. Huntington lost just twice that season in 25 games.

Education

Marshall College was granted university status by the West Virginia legislature.

Retail

Blue laws left some employees of Huntington discount stores seeing red — and demanding green.

Three employees of Heck's discount store who had been arrested in "blue law" raids sued managers of three other stores, the Huntington Store, J.C. Penney, and Sears, store for $50,000 each.

The store officials had sworn out warrants for the arrest of 13 employees of Heck's discount store for allegedly violating the state's blue law, which prohibited businesses from operating on Sundays. Heck's, apparently, had ignored that prohibition, and the rival store managers started pointing fingers — leading to the raids and arrests.

Blue laws were serious business.

Even Santa got cited for violating a blue law in a Philadelphia suburb after passing out gifts to children on a Sunday.

More raids followed in Huntington, and before long, other Huntington employees had filed similar lawsuits, bringing the total amount of damages sought to $500,000.

Meanwhile, a grand jury was considering charges against 40 employees arrested at three different stores: 19 at Heck's, 18 at The Bazaar, and three at Whiz Discount Store. The indictments were dismissed, but indictments against Heck's and The Bazaar were allowed to stand.

Stores that observed the blue laws weren't happy at being forced to close on Sundays while competitors ignored the statute. But some customers were equally perturbed at being unable to buy clothing or shoes on that day — even though bowling alleys and taverns were allowed to remain open.

"Why don't you close down the beer parlors on Sunday before you close down this place?" a woman shouted as police officers arrested employees at a discount store one Sunday.

Movie theaters were allowed to stay open, too, under the law, which was more than a century old and had been reaffirmed in 1959.

It stated:

"If any person, on a Sabbath day, be found laboring at any trade or calling, or employ his minor children, apprentices, or servants in labor or other business, except in household or other work of necessity or charity, he shall be guilty of a misdemeanor."

The fine, if convicted, was $15, which didn't sound like much, but it would be something like $135 in 2021. But arresting people risked incurring lawsuits, as the cases in Huntington demonstrated.

Of the 13 suits that were filed in Huntington, eight wound up being settled out of court, and a jury awarded $2,000 in another. Four were still pending a year later.

A postcard shows the UpTowner Inn's neon sign, welcoming visitors to Huntington. *Author collection*

1962

Lodging

The UpTowner Inn couldn't really decide whether it wanted to be a hotel or a motel. Maybe that's why it settled on the name "Inn."

It looked like an oversized motel, a sprawling four-story

structure with three arms that stretched out in different directions with 144 guest rooms. And it had exterior walkways like a motel, too. But, like a hotel, it was located in the heart of the city, on 4th Avenue.

The inn cost $1.3 million to build and was one of a few UpTowners that went up in West Virginia around the same time. One opened in Clarksburg, and another in Parkersburg (just a year after the Huntington inn debuted).

The UpTowner opened with a bang: It served as headquarters for the Miss USA pageant. After Jo Ann Odum won the previous year's pageant, Huntington got to host this time around.

Teen idol Frankie Avalon, known for his No. 1 hit "Venus" and soon to appear in a series of *Beach Party* movies, was tabbed to serve as one of the judges, and the UpTowner provided rooms to its 44 contestants and pageant staff.

The week of festivities included three dances, a river cruise, a Marshall football game, and a golf tournament. There was even a parade down 4th Avenue that drew a crowd of 20,000 to watch the contestants and a line of 85 cars, six floats, and 10 high school bands pass by.

The crown did not stay in West Virginia, though: Amedee Chabot from California took the prize.

In its later years, the UpTowner underwent renovations that made it more like a hotel. For a time, it became a Holiday Inn. It finally closed in 2002 when Holiday Inn opened a new hotel up the street, and the Uptowner was converted into apartments called the Flats on 4th.

Finally, in 2018, it was demolished.

As a footnote, however, the UpTowner in Parkersburg survived, despite having closed in 1987. The building was purchased by Marriott and underwent a wholesale transformation to become TownePlace Suites.

Roller Skating

The Roll-A-Rama skating rink opened.

1963

Auto Racing

NASCAR was coming to Huntington. Well, just east of town, really — to the tiny community of Ona.

The Mountaineer 300, the first NASCAR Grand National points race in the Mountain State, kicked off racing at the new $750,000 West Virginia International Speedway on Aug. 16, and you could reserve your tickets for $6.

The 7/16-mile oval was ready and waiting for NASCAR's best drivers. Among those in the field for the first Mountaineer 300 were Richard Petty and Ned Jarrett, both of whom were in the thick of the battle for the points championship with Joe Weatherly.

David Pearson was also entered. West Virginian Bud Harless would be driving a Pontiac. And 38-year-old "Fearless" Freddy Lorenzen of Charlotte, the nation's top stock-car money winner with $90,000 in his pocket for the season, was entered, too. He'd be competing with the others for a top prize of $1,600.

The grandstand seated 10,000, but a lot more than that turned out for the inaugural race: 16,000 to be exact.

Lorenzen stayed in the race after clipping the wall at one point and beat out Weatherly for the checkered flag, with Jim Paschall of High Point, North Carolina, third and Jarett fourth. Petty led for a portion of the race before his car started to smoke and he lost 5 minutes in the pits, winding up 10th. But he'd be back.

So would NASCAR.

In fact, there were big plans still for the site. A

superspeedway with a 1.375-mile track was planned that would have encircled the original track, with 30,000 seats. The original backstretch wall was even built.

But complications soon followed.

Wendell Scott (the first Black driver to win a NASCAR Cup race), Bobby Allison, and eventual winner Richard Petty circle the speedway track at Ona in 1971. *JGarrett71, Creative Commons 4.0*

A sought-after interstate ramp that would have provided direct access to the track was denied. And although NASCAR returned for a 500-lap race in 1964, the pavement cracked during the event, leading to complaints from the drivers. With attendance down to 12,000, NASCAR decided not to return in '65, and the superspeedway plans were scuttled.

For the record, Petty won the 1964 race, then won twice more at Ona when NASCAR revisited the track after it was purchased by Dick Clark of *American Bandstand* fame in 1969. Petty won the 300-mile race in 1970 before a crowd of 8,600, but there were more problems when the lights went out and the drivers (without headlights) were totally in the dark.

NASCAR returned with a 500-lap race that drew 10,000

people in '71.

Petty won again.

And Bobby Allison won a Grand National East Series race there in 1972, but that was the end of big-time NASCAR racing at Ona.

The track also served as a concert venue, hosting the Summers On Festival celebrating "freedom, peace, love and good rock music." Grand Funk Railroad was the headliner for the 1970 show, and other acts on the bill were Zephyr, Bloodrock, Dreams, and two West Virginia bands: Heavy Rain and Quiet.

Bowling

A new 24-lane bowling center called Imperial Lanes opened during the summer.

It would close in 2005.

Civil Rights

With a name like the White Pantry, it should have come as no surprise that the restaurant would become a flashpoint for civil rights protests. The only surprise might be that it took so long.

The first lunch counter sit-in had taken place in 1960 at the Woolworth in Greensboro, North Carolina, spearheaded by four university students there. When the protests finally reached Huntington, university students who took the lead there, too.

The struggle hadn't been easy in other places, and it wasn't in Huntington, either.

In July, a multiracial group of about 25 students from Marshall and West Virginia State College led by Black attorney Herbert Harrison staged a sit-in at the White Pantry, both at the counter and in some of the booths, before the manager responded by closing the restaurant entirely for the day.

It wasn't the first place the group had targeted.

They had already succeeded in getting Bailey's Cafeteria to drop its policy against serving people of color. Bailey's, founded by Morris and Sadie Bailey, had been open since 1934, initially in the basement of the Fifth Avenue Hotel and later on the 400 block of 9th Street. Their nephew, the manager there, initially resisted integrating because he feared alienating white customers.

Protesters responded by getting in line, Black and white students together; the cafeteria servers refused to serve the Black patrons, but they just joined their white companions at a table and all ate the food the white students had ordered. After a series of back-and-forth court actions, Bailey's finally relented in the late spring and allowed integrated dining.

But the fight wasn't over yet.

It just shifted to the White Pantry.

After being turned away the first time, the protesters returned. But the restaurant owner upped the ante Aug. 5 by burning sulfur cakes, spraying insecticide, and turning up the heat inside the restaurant to make things as uncomfortable as he could for those seeking to stage the new sit-in.

Things then got even more heated when the attorney, Henderson, and restaurant owner Roba Quesenberry got into a shoving match after Henderson heard that a woman had been thrown bodily out of the Pantry.

"I went to the place and as I put my hand on the door knob, he pushed me back, and I instinctively pushed him back," Henderson said.

Phil Carter, a 6-foot-3 Marshall student who had played basketball for the Thundering Herd, was among the protesters. He wasn't a newcomer to making his feelings known: As a teen, he had often walked into the Clarksburg theater and sat in the whites-only section on the floor rather than the balcony reserved for Black patrons. Then, they'd throw him out.

"For a long time, I would not go because of that," he said of the theater's segregated policy. "When I was 16, I did go, and I went to the main floor and if they had to throw my out, they just had to throw me out."

When he joined the group protesting at the white pantry, he and the others pledged themselves to non-violent protest. But their determination was tested by Quesenberry's tough tactics: In addition to the insecticide and sulfur cakes, he mopped the floors with ammonia.

A cattle prod was even used on Carter.

"It took every bit of non-violent willpower in the individuals to restrain themselves from retaliating," Carter admitted.

The next time, instead of burning sulfur or spraying insecticide, Quesenberry locked the doors when protesters showed up. But that created a problem when one of the customers inside needed to leave. The door opened, and the protesters tried to keep it open so they could enter, while white men inside tried to close it. Still, four protesters managed to make it inside — only to be asked by three police officers to leave when Quesenberry said he was closing.

He reopened when the group left to march through downtown, then closed again when they returned.

It was almost like a game of chicken.

But it was no game.

Quesenberry was adamant he wouldn't let Black people into his establishment unless the law required him to do so. One protest leader, meanwhile, promised to "fill the jails up" if police arrested more protesters. Quesenberry went to court in an attempt to stop the protests, but a lower court ruled that demonstrators could picket outside the White Pantry.

Then, finally, a year later, Quesenberry dropped his appeal of that ruling in light of what he called "national developments."

He didn't say what those developments were, but they most likely involved the Civil Rights Act of 1964. The new law outlawed discrimination, but that didn't mean Quesenberry was ready to serve people of color. Even when the law required that he do so, he maintained that it "did not dictate how I cook" and served them raw bacon and eggs or undercooked meat in an attempt to discourage their patronage.

Jim Crow might have been dealt a blow, but racism was far from dead.

Crime

Burglars got away with $7,000 from the Whiz Discount Store safe.

Whiz was a Huntington-based chain with stores on U.S. 60, 5th Avenue, and 3rd Avenue. It had a catchy slogan: "Whiz: The Best Store There Is," and carried just about anything you could hope to find, from groceries to garden equipment. You could buy your fishing or hunting license there, too.

1964

Fast Food

Frank Volk launched the submarine when he opened his new sandwich shop at 1521 4th Ave. in August — the submarine sandwich, that is.

He opened a year before Subway got its start in Bridgeport, Connecticut, and Huntington had never seen anything like what he had on the menu. There were burger joints and hot dog stands, but sub sandwiches (also known as hoagies in the Philadelphia area) were a new kind of fast-food delicacy.

Volk had to order the bread from out of state, because not a single bakery in West Virginia made hoagie rolls.

Volk, a former restaurant equipment salesman from Baltimore, served a popular steak sandwich, prepared in butter on a flat-top grill, which he seasoned with cayenne pepper and finely chopped-up cherry peppers. He called it a steak sandwich with "hots."

Volk opened a second shop, at 3rd Avenue and 13th Street in the early eighties, but Frank's Sandwich Shop never became another subway. Both locations closed in the nineties, and the original was replaced by a drive-in auto claims center.

Faith

A crowd of 12,000 gathered at Fairfield Stadium to hear evangelist Billy Graham preach.

1965

Athletics

Marshall athletics adopted "Thundering Herd" as its nickname. The school's teams had been referred to by that name for some time, but they'd also been known as "Big Green." In a vote of students and faculty on Jan. 5, "Thundering Herd" defeated "Big Green" and "Rams" to become the official choice.

1967

Recreation

Camden Park had a trio of new rides for parkgoers in '67: the Paratrooper, Jolly Caterpillar, and German Carousel. These went along with favorites like the Big Dipper rollercoaster, Turnpike Ride (gasoline-powered cars on a miniature turnpike), and Ferris wheel.

The entrance sign to Camden Park. *Author photo*

Retail

The Pied Piper music store started in a small shop on 4th Avenue owned by a pair of brothers, Chuck and Larry Levine, who advertised their store by putting drums out on the second-floor balcony. But it soon grew into something much bigger.

The brothers' original building was demolished in 1976 to make way for a parking lot, so they just upsized, building a 15,000-square-foot store in a Tudor-style building at 3rd Avenue and Veterans Memorial Boulevard. The building covered the entire block and even included an amphitheater with room for 150 people.

The Levines didn't just sell musical instruments (everything from pianos down to pennywhisles). They sold stereos and stereo equipment, too, carrying brands like Sony, Vega, JVC, and Teac. And they opened other stores to become a chain that ranked as the third-largest of its kind by *Music Trends Magazine* in 1991.

Larry Levine died in 2002, and the Pied Piper went out of business that same year.

1968

MEMORIAL FIELD HOUSE
Huntington, W. Va.
WEDNESDAY, MAY 15 – 7:30 P.M.

THE CREAM
THE GRASS ROOTS

Plus
Added Attractions
THE KICKIN' MUSTANGS
THE PURPLE REIGN
Prices: $4.50 — $3.50 — $2.50

Buy advance tickets at Kay's Jewelry Store, Ninth St., Huntington, W. Va., The Record Shop, Ashland, Ky., Dick's Record Shop, Marton, O., The Record Shop, Portsmouth, O., Music Shop, Milton and Hurricane, W. Va.
Tickets will be sold at Memorial Field House, Huntington, W. Va., two hours before performance.

Music

Talk about a double-bill: Supergroup Cream, featuring guitar god Eric Clapton, drummer Ginger Baker, and vocalist/bassist Jack Bruce, was coming to town for a gig at the Memorial Fieldhouse May 15. That would have been enough to make any rock fan sit up and take notice.

But also taking the stage were the Grass Roots, who had a pair of top-10 hits to their credit in "Let's Live for Today" and "Midnight Confessions." (They'd have a third in 1971 with "Sooner or Later.")

Two local bands — The Kickin' Mustangs and the Purple Reign — rounded out the evening's entertainment. Tickets were $4.50, $3.50, or $2.50 each.

1969

Basketball

Huntington High suffered just two losses during a 26-game season, and the championship game wasn't one of them. The Pony Express rolled past the Oak Hill Red Devils 75-57 to wrap up the state title.

Greg Hawkins, a 6-foot-5 senior, led the way with 29 points and six assists. He was perfect on nine free-throw attempts, running his tournament streak to 20 in a row and setting a record in the process.

The game was won on the boards, with the Pony Express gathering in 68 rebounds to just 32 for Oak Hill.

A City in Mourning

1970–1979

1970

Milestones

Huntington lost 11 percent of its population — and 11,000 people — dipping to just over 74,000.

Tragedy

Just like that, the Marshall University football team was gone.

But memories remain and tears still flow for the 75 people who died on November 14, 1970 in the deadliest plane crash in NCAA history.

The 1970 season was supposed to be a comeback story. The Thundering Herd had gone through the 1967 and '68 seasons without a single victory, and the team had been suspended from the Mid-American Conference for recruiting violations and "woefully inadequate facilities." The NCAA added to the burden with one year of probation.

The program was within one game of setting a record for futility when is ran its winless streak to 27 games before winning three of its last four to close out 1969. Coach Rick Tolley was optimistic about the future.

"We've begun to turn our program around," he said. "We're heading in the right direction."

Then the 1970 season began with a narrow 17-14 loss to East Carolina in Kingston, North Carolina, and even though it was an "L," it was clear that Marshall had become competitive again. Things were looking up.

Then came the flight home.

It was supposed to be a short one: just 40 minutes from Kingston back to Huntington. But the twin-engine Southern Airways plane was flying too low as it approached its destination.

In fact, it was flying 300 feet below the normal altitude, shearing off treetops in the fog and rain as it approached Tri-State Airport. It never reached the landing strip, though, skimming two small hills, its engines becoming clogged with tree branches as it plunged into a mist-covered, wooded ravine.

"As the plane kept hitting larger trees, it became more impossible to recover for a safe landing," said John Reed, chairman of the National Transportation Safety Board.

The aircraft exploded on impact, still a mile and a half from the airport, and everyone on board was burned beyond recognition. It took more than 12 hours to remove all the bodies from the wreckage. The toll included 36 football players, five coaches — including Tolley, who was just 30 years old — the team trainer, and all five members of the airplane crew.

Nearly 60 children were left as orphans.

Twenty-five team boosters, some of them among Huntington's most prominent residents, also perished.

"The whole fabric, the whole heart of the town was aboard," one resident later said.

1971

Transportation

The Mud River Covered Bridge, built in 1875, was restored and moved to a temporary site near its original location. It was moved again, in 1997, to the Cabell County Fairgrounds in Milton, east of Huntington.

1972

Basketball

Marshall's men's team lost just four times in 27 games behind an offense that averaged 92.4 points a game, eighth-best in the country.

The Thundering Herd, playing as an independent, finished the season ranked No. 12 in the nation but lost to Louisiana 112-101 in the first round of the NCAA Tournament.

1973

Retail

A deal was in the works to build an enclosed mall on a two-block parcel of land for $20 million. The mall on 3rd Avenue between 8th and 10th streets was intended to house two anchor department stores and 50 specialty shops.

The "superblock" project was supposed to be 18 months away, but it would take a lot longer than that for the land to be developed. The developer couldn't find tenants for the proposed indoor mall and wound up filing bankruptcy.

The most that ever came of it was the construction of the Huntington Civic Center at the west end in 1977. But at various points in time, plans for an outlet center, office tower, and off-track casino all fell through.

In the meantime, one block over, 4th Avenue had become a haven for teenage cruisers to tie up traffic after dark.

The solution?

Mayor Buddy Nelson had the city spend $7,000 to create a two-lane paved strip on the vacant superblock where kids could hang out without blocking regular traffic. They called it Cruise Avenue, but critics referred to it derisively as "Bruise Avenue" because of the fights that broke out there, accompanied by those timeless teen preoccupations: drinking and drugs.

The strip was open from 6 to midnight on Fridays and Saturdays, but some cruisers gathered there during the week, as well.

Eventually, in 2004, the roadway was torn up and a shopping, dining, and entertainment site called Pullman Square opened there. ...

But when it's said that Huntington didn't have an indoor mall at that point, it's not entirely true. Also in 1973, the East Hills Mall opened on U.S. 60 east of town at the 29th Street interchange, featuring a Hills department store and A&P supermarket as its anchors.

The Hills store was the chain's seventh in West Virginia, with 80,000 square feet of space and 74 departments. It was a largely regional chain, having been founded in Youngstown in 1957 before spreading to neighboring states.

Initially a traditional store, Hills evolved over the years into a discount department store that, by 1987, would be the nation's eighth-largest discount retailer.

The A&P, meanwhile, was the last outlet in that chain to open in Huntington and also the last to close: By 1985, it was gone.

At just 111,000 square feet, however, the shopping center wasn't the kind of large-scale megamall that was opening around the country around that time. It was limited in scope, and that may have discouraged shoppers from making the trip to patronize its stores.

It never had more than about a dozen tenants lining its narrow indoor gallery of shops, and these came and went in a stream as if through a revolving door. The tenants at one time or another included a King's Table smorgasbord restaurant, Fitness

World, Huntington School of Beauty, Sights 'n Sounds music store, a jewelry store, bookstore, shoe store, and bank.

Even lower rents failed to attract tenants to the mall during the eighties, and it was turned into an office park in 2008.

1975

Retail

The Big Bear supermarket chain had been a part of the Huntington landscape for 16 years when it introduced something a little different: a Harts Family Center store at 3100 U.S. Route 60 East.

Harts opened in a space formerly occupied by Arlan's Department Store, which had recently gone out of business. Harts offered products like clothing, shoes, jewelry, bedding, electronics, and housewares.

Originally, Harts had been a separate chain that operated in the basement of a couple of Big Bear Markets. But Big Bear had purchased it outright in 1954 and started opening up Harts outlets in locations vacated by other stores (such as the Arlan's) or adjacent its new supermarkets.

Big Bear would open another Harts next to its own supermarket in 1976 at the new Ceredo Plaza shopping center, and another Big Bear and Harts in 1981 in the old Sears building at 5th Avenue and 29th Street, which had just vacated by the department store so it could move to the new Huntington Mall.

Just after that, though, it closed the freestanding store in the old Arlan's amid declining revenues. Big Bear would later abandon the Harts concept altogether in favor of superstores it called Big Bear Plus. ...

Speaking of the Ceredo Plaza, plans for the new shopping center came into focus with the sale of land where the Ceredo Drive-In had been operating. The family that had owned it since before it was used for greyhound racing agreed to sell it to a developer, and the Town of Ceredo issued $3 million worth of bonds to pay for the construction.

It wasn't the first time a shopping center had been proposed for the site. Way back in 1959, a Pittsburgh group had sought to build a $2 million, 200,000-square-foot center with parking for 2,000 cars. But that plan never got off the ground.

This one did, though.

The first phase of Ceredo Plaza consisted of the area's second Big Bear market and some other shops. More space was added over the next couple of years, and more businesses moved in. Among the early tenants were a beauty salon, video rental store, crafts store, restaurants, and a nutrition store.

Oh, and there was a veterinary clinic, too, an ironic addition to a site where greyhound racing had once been held.

1976

Baseball

The Pony Express rode back to the pinnacle of high school baseball in West Virginia, downing Morgantown 4-3 for the AAA championship.

Football

Fairfield Stadium was showing its age, but more room was needed, so it was expanded to seat 18,000 fans for football. The team wouldn't exactly be a great drawing card for the next seven seasons, posting losing records each year. But the Herd would soon be packing 'em in.

1977

The Huntington Civic Center opened in 1977. *Wv funnyman, Creative Commons 4.0*

Community

The Huntington Civic Center opened on 3rd Avenue, including an arena with seating for 9,000 and a 15,000-foot conference center that was the largest in the state. (The arena was later named the Big Sandy Superstore Arena).

The arena was supposed to make a big splash from the outset. Elvis Presley was booked to perform there in the third week of September, a week after it opened. Unfortunately, Presley passed away a month before the scheduled show.

The arena has hosted the likes of John Denver, Bon Jovi, Merle Haggard, the Beach Boys, Conway Twitty, and George Jones. ...

The first phase of Harris Riverfront Park was completed, consisting of a boat-launch ramp, marina area, "comfort station" and parking. An amphitheater would be added in 1983, along with more green space, another comfort station, and a lower walkway.

The project, named for David W. Harris, the city's former director of urban renewal, was completed in 1997. Total cost: $6.6 million.

Rocco's Little Italy on 4th Avenue in Huntington. *Author photo*

Dining

Rocco Muriale had already been in the restaurant business for eight years by the time the opened Rocco's Ristorante. He started working at Muriale's in Fairmont, West Virginia, a restaurant founded by his parents and his uncle, in 1969.

But then, in 1977, the Army veteran struck out on his own and founded Rocco's Ristorante.

Muriale credited his friend Frank Lucente, with whom he later founded Sam's Hot Dog Stand, and Frank's wife Betty with encouraging him to open his own place, which he described as "the hardest decision of my life." The pair both had a stake in Rocco's until 1989, when Muriale took sole ownership while Lucente took over Sam's.

Rocco's Ristorante is in Ceredo, up the road just beyond Camden Park. In 2001, Muriale purchased a building in Huntington that had been the home to Ward's Donut Shop for decades. He rechristened it Rocco's Little Italy.

1978

Sen. Robert C. Byrd, left, meets with then-President Jimmy Carter, who holds Byrd's 1978 album, an unexpected hit in Huntington. *Public domain*

Music

West Virginia's Robert Byrd, the minority leader in the U.S. Senate, had a hit on his hands. A record album titled *U.S. Senator Robert Byrd, Mountain Fiddler* was flying off the shelves at Davidson's Record Shop in Huntington.

Just before Christmas, Mac McGlynn of Davidson's said the record had hit No. 12 on the shop's Top 25 list: "This is the first time I can remember an album made by a West Virginian making our bestseller list."

The distributor said they'd sold 500 or 600 copies already at that point, and business was brisk at the National Record Mart in Huntington, too.

"It doesn't compare to our bestsellers, since we specialize in rock and country, but it's selling very well right now," manager Kim Watts said. "We've had to order and reorder. I think a lot of people are buying the album for their collection."

Byrd was backed on the record by a group called The Country Gentleman. His was also selling well at Dr. Feel Good's Record Emporium in Barboursville, where bluegrass music was among the specialties.

Jon Courts of Dr. Feel Good's, who called it "a superb album."

"We got about 10 calls a day asking about it before it came out," he said. "He's done a great job of getting it to the public. I don't like to hear a trained voice singing bluegrass. The music is sung from the soul, and I think Sen. Byrd does a decent job."

The record might have been what Watts described as "a novelty item," but Byrd was anything but a one-hit wonder as a legislator. In fact, he outlasted the phonograph record altogether and was still in office long after the iPod made its debut.

Byrd remains the longest-serving U.S. senator, having spent 51 years in the Senate until his death in 2019 at the age of 92.

1979

Music

Kiss, the rock band with the face paint and a reputation for spitting fire and blood in bombastic concerts, stopped at Huntington Civic Center on a tour to promote their latest album, *Dynasty*. The setlist, however, only included a couple of songs from that album: the top-10 hit "I Was Made for Lovin' You" and their cover of the Rolling Stones' "2000 Man."

The band would return, with two different members, in 1988 to promote their album *Crazy Nights*, with Ted Nugent as the supporting act.

Rise of the Herd

1980–1989

1980

Baseball

The eighties belonged to Huntington East on the baseball diamond. The Highlanders captured the first of three consecutive state titles to kick off the decade with a 4-0 win over Woodrow Wilson in the AAA title game.

They followed that up with a 10-1 win over Oak Hill in 1981 and a 3-2 victory over Martinsburg in 1982.

After a brief respite, they returned to the top of the heap in 1986 with an 8-6 win over Lewis County and capped their string of five championships in eight years with a 6-2 triumph over Parkersburg South in 1987.

Milestones

For the second decade in a row, Huntington lost about 11,000 people, with just 63,684 residing within the city limits following a 14.3 percent decline.

1981

Baseball

Huntington native Steve Yeager, catcher for the Los Angeles Dodgers, shared World Series MVP honors with two teammates as the team defeated the New York Yankees in the World Series 4 games to 2.

Yeager hit a double and two home runs in the series, including the game-winning homer in Game 5. Known more for his defense than his bat, he wound up playing 15 seasons in the big leagues, including 14 with the Dodgers.

If his last name seems familiar, yes, he is related to Chuck Yeager (his cousin), the first pilot to break the sound barrier. Chuck Yeager was born in Myra, West Virginia, less than an hour's drive from Huntington. Charleston's airport is named in his honor.

Steve Yeager, Los Angeles Dodgers catcher and Huntington native. *Public domain*

Health Care

Phase III of the Cabell Huntington Hospital's master plan was executed with the help of a $9 million bond. The hospital added a 26-bed critical care floor along with nurseries for healthy and ICU babies, and made other improvements in areas such as dialysis, as well.

Retail

The area's first enclosed shopping center, Huntington Mall, opened in Barboursville, east of Huntington, with Sears, J.C. Penney, Lazarus, and Stone & Thomas as anchors.

Penney's moved from the downtown location where it had been since the 1930s, while Sears relocated from its standalone location at 5th Avenue and 29th Street. Stone & Thomas already operated a store downtown, while Lazarus was new to the city.

The mall also included a six-screen movie theater operated by General Cinemas, which was torn down in 2008 and replaced by a 12-screen theater on the same site.

Tennis player Bobby Riggs, famous for his "Battle of the Sexes" matches against Billie Jean King and Margaret Court, appeared at the opening of the Foot Locker store there.

Phar-Mor pharmacy would join the mall as a fifth anchor in 1990, though it would close 12 years later.

1983

Fast Food

Hot dogs were still popular in Huntington: popular enough, in fact, to support another hot dog stand. This one, Sam's, opened at 816 8th St.

Frank Lucente, a Marshall University graduate student had gotten hooked on frozen hot dogs from Chick's Confectionery in his hometown of Fairmont, West Virginia. He'd pick up a dozen of them whenever he went home to visit, then he'd freeze them and take them back to school.

Eventually, he decided just to open up his own hot dog stand in Huntington, and — since the sauce was always a huge attraction — hoped Chick's would share its recipe with him. The owner turned him down cold, saying he would "take it to the grave" with him.

Undeterred, Frank tracked down the woman who'd given Chick's the recipe in the first place. She was still living in Fairmont and selling the sauce at her church bazaar. Chick's had altered the recipe slightly, but she let him have the original, which he used as the basis for a sauce he developed with his friend Rocco Muriale of Rocco's Ristorante, with whom he co-owned Sam's.

They named the place after their fathers, both of whom, coincidentally, were named Sam. (It was also Muriale's middle name.)

Lucente took sole ownership of the business in 1989, while Muriale became sole owner of Rocco's. He eventually started selling franchises and expanded to some 45 locations in West Virginia, Virginia, Kentucky, North Carolina, and Georgia. Two of them are in Huntington, at 4450 Piedmont Rd. and 2885 5th Ave.

Football

The Marshall University football team ended a string of 19 straight losing seasons — including five in which it had one or zero wins — with a 6-5 record in their first of two seasons under Stan Parrish. They would follow that up with a 7-3-1 mark in 1985, but that was just the beginning of much better things to come.

Recreation

Camden Park marked its 80th anniversary by adding a log flume ride.

1984

Business

Bill Spurlock had spent two decades in the real estate business when he decided to shift gears and start selling automobiles.

When he opened Bill Spurlock Dodge on the corner of 4th Avenue at 4th Street, he was a late arrival to Huntington's Automobile Row, a three-block stretch of car dealerships that ran along 4th Avenue from the building where Spurlock set up shop all the way down to 7th Street.

Two auto dealerships still in business on 4th Avenue in Huntington, once a hotbed of car sales: Bill Spurlock Dodge, top, and Southern Motors, above. *Author photos*

The strip of auto dealerships had seen its heyday from the 1920s through the 1960s. Their numbers included the Huntington Motor Company, where you could buy Studebakers; Galligher Motors Sales for Lincoln and Mercury models; and the Thackston dealership, which sold General Motors cars.

Bruce Perry Motors had a selection of cars you won't find for sale anymore, such as DeSotos, Auburns, and Plymouths.

They're all gone today.

On another section of 4th Avenue, across from the Greyhound Station, a small dealership called Southern Motors was still operating. A sign on the side of a small cinderblock building proclaimed that it had been in business since 1947.

Bill Spurlock, meanwhile, died in 2017. But his company remained in business, providing one last lingering look at an area of Huntington once devoted to the sale of the automobile.

Football

Inspectors found that the stands on the east side of Fairfield Stadium were at risk of collapse, leading to their demolition.

Aluminum bleachers replaced them.

But eventually, half-measures were no longer enough to sustain the aging stadium. It was finally torn down completely in 2004.

1985

Transportation

The East Huntington Bridge, a modern 900-foot-long cable-stayed span across the Ohio River, opened to link Huntington with Proctorville, Ohio. Work on the bridge began in 1983 and was completed in August, at a cost of $38 million.

Designed by Arvid Grant and Associates of Olympia,

Washington, it was the first bridge of its kind in West Virginia. It was renamed in 2006 to honor, Frank Gatski former center for the Cleveland Browns who became Marshall University's first pro football Hall of Famer and who had died the previous year.

The East Huntington Bridge was completed in 1985. *Carol M. Highsmith, Library of Congress*

1987

Basketball

Marshall rolled to the Southern Conference men's basketball title with a 15-1 record and a 25-6 overall mark, qualifying for the NCAA Tournament. The Thundering Herd dropped a first-round game to Texas Christian, 76-60.

Skip Henderson led the Herd in scoring with 21 points a game, and Rodney Holden was the conference leader in rebounds.

Football

The Thundering Herd made it all the way to the Division I-AA championship game as the No. 14 seed, and had victory in their sights against No. 2 seed Northeast Louisiana.

Marshall went ahead 42-28 with 36 seconds left in the third quarter thanks to a 6-yard touchdown run by Ronald Darby. But future San Diego Chargers quarterback Stan Humphries engineered a comeback in the fourth quarter, accounting for all but one of NLU's points with a 10-yard scoring pass, a two-point conversion pass, and a 3-yard touchdown run.

When the dust cleared, NLU had eked out a 43-42 victory and kept Marshall from claiming its first national championship.

For now.

Transportation

A new $5.8 million bridge opened in November on U.S. 60 across the Big Sandy River between Kenova and Catlettsburg, Kentucky.

It was a boon to residents on both sides of the river, with Kentucky residents now able to buy beer outside the city limits of their "dry" town and West Virginians able to buy cigarettes easily in Kentucky — for $2 a carton less.

Catlettsburg Mayor Arthur Porter joked about it with his Kenova counterpart Frank Heck: "I told Frank I would bring him a carton of cigarettes and he could bring me a six-pack of beer, but we thought better of it. But really, that would have said a lot about the importance of this bridge."

The bridge, which replaced an older span, included a covered pedestrian walkway designed to let children walk safely from Kentucky to the Dreamland Pool in Kenova.

"It's a wonder to me that somebody hasn't been seriously injured on that old bridge," Heck said. "The walkway will be covered with a chain-link fence so nobody can throw anything off the bridge and nobody will be in danger of falling off."

1988

Basketball

Huntington High returned to the top of the basketball heap for the first time in nearly two decades, polishing off Martinsburg in a high-scoring thriller 91-88. Huntington wrapped up its season with a 25-2 mark.

Music

The Ragtime Lounge hired a new group to be its house band.

The singer, from neighboring Kentucky, was a man named Billy Ray Cyrus. And the Ragtime Lounge was the first place he performed what would become his signature song in 1991.

Immediately after recording the song, Cyrus said, he and his band "started playing it that night at the Ragtime Lounge in Huntington, West Virginia. The audience immediately gravitated to it and wanted to hear it again and again. I think we played it four times that night."

Billy Ray Cyrus first sang "Achy Breaky Heart" in Huntington. *Public domain*

"Achy Breaky Heart" would be Cyrus' debut single off his album *Some Gave All*. It shot straight to the top of the Billboard Hot Country Songs chart, where it spent five weeks, longer than any other debut single since 1967. It also reached, No. 3 in the UK, and No. 4 on the Billboard Hot 100.

And Huntington heard it live first.

1989

Football

Marshall University's Board of Regents gave the go-ahead to $70 million bond sale, including $30 million to finance a new football stadium that was supposed to hold 30,000 seats. But when the then-unnamed stadium opened on Sept. 7, 1991, there was only room for 28,000 because the stadium seats were larger than the room allotted.

Gridiron Supremacy

1990-1999

Marshall's new football stadium opened in 1991. *Author photo*

1990

Baseball

Huntington hadn't had a baseball team in nearly half a century, but it got a new one in 1990 when the Huntington Cubs began play in the Appalachian League.

The Cubs played at St. Cloud Commons, at 19th Street and Jackson Avenue, and did all right in their first season, finishing second with a record of 40-29. Dave Stevens didn't have a particularly distinguished season on the mound, finishing 2-4, but would go on to pitch seven seasons in the majors.

Their inaugural season turned out to be the Cubs' best. They never topped the .500 mark in any of their next four seasons, which marked the end of Huntington's run in the Appalachian League.

Football

Marshall played its last football game at Fairfield Stadium, losing to Eastern Kentucky 15-12 on Nov. 10.

Milestones

Huntington's population was barely what it had been in 1920 following a drop of nearly 14 percent, standing at 54,844. Charleston remained the state's largest city with about 2,400 more, but it, too, was shrinking, and so was Wheeling, which now had fewer than 35,000.

1991

Football

Marshall played for the first time in its new 28,000-seat football stadium and made it a memorable experience for the fans, coming away with a 24-23 win over New Hampshire.

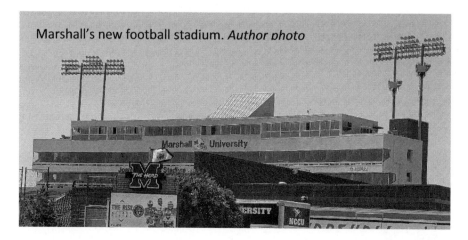

Marshall's new football stadium. *Author photo*

The Thundering Herd won every game they played at home in their first year at the stadium, making it all the way to the Division I-AA championship game before losing 25-17 to Youngstown State.

Music

Jane's Addiction played the Huntington Civic Center on May 8 as part of their spring tour of North America. The band had released its top-20 album *Ritual de lo habitual* the previous year, featuring the back-to-back alternative No. 1 hits "Stop!" and "Been Caught Stealing."

1992

Football

After falling short against Youngstown in the Division I-AA title game the year before, Marshall got its revenge with a 31-28 victory over the same team in a championship rematch.

The Thundering Herd opened up a 28-0 lead with less than 6 minutes left in the third quarter, then had to hold off a furious rally by YSU that tied the score at 28 with 2:28 to play. But Marshall got the last laugh, winning on a 22-yard field goal by Willy Merrick with 7 ticks remaining on the clock.

The Herd finished the season with an 11-2-1 record.

1993

Ice Hockey

The Huntington Blizzard made its debut in the East Coast Hockey League, playing at the Huntington Civic Center.

The first season wasn't memorable, as the Blizzard posted a

record of 14-49, and while the team improved, it only managed to make the playoffs three times in its seven years of existence. The Blizzard's most successful season was its final one, when it posted its best record (35-25) and made it to the second round of the playoffs.

Jim Bermingham, a wing from Montreal, played six seasons with the Blizzard, finishing as Huntington's all-time leader in goals with 172, assists with 282, and points with 454. Kelly Harper from Sudbury, Ontario, played those same six seasons (1994-2000), and finished second in each of those categories, playing the most games of any Huntington player at 356.

The Blizzard averaged better than 3,700 fans in each of their first two seasons, but attendance dropped off after that, ranging between 2,100 and 2,600 for the final four seasons. The franchise was dormant for four seasons before being reborn in 2003 as the Texas Wildcatters.

1995

Baseball

After the Huntington Cubs ended their run in the Appalachian League, the city found a replacement in the River City Rumblers, who finished with the worst record in the league.

Attendance was near the bottom, too, and the team ceased operations after a single year. Only one member of the roster, pitcher Julio Manon, ever made it to the majors, seeing limited duty with the Montreal Expos in 2003 and the Baltimore Orioles three years later.

Transportation

The old 6th Street Bridge over the Ohio River was done. A set of simultaneous explosions ripped the 400-foot center span into pieces and sent it crashing into the water below, ending 69 years of service.

Its replacement, the Robert C. Byrd Bridge, was already in place, having been opened to traffic the previous October. The $32.6 million span connected Huntington with Chesapeake, Ohio across the water.

The new Robert C. Byrd Bridge. *Author photo*

Byrd clearly liked the new bridge better than the old one, which he declared "a calamity waiting to happen."

The spires from the old 6th Street Bridge were preserved, and two are displayed along 9th Street between 3rd and 5th avenues in Huntington.

1996

Education

Old Huntington High School's last class graduated. The school was merged with Huntington East High School into a new Huntington High. The old Pony Express nickname was abandoned, and Huntington East's Highlanders name was preserved for the new combined school.

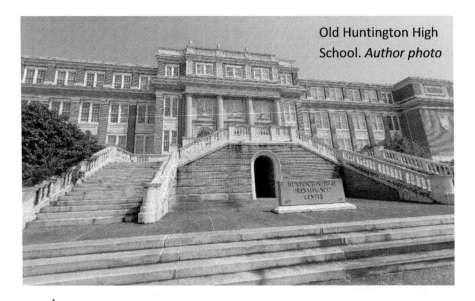

Old Huntington High School. *Author photo*

Football

Marshall left Division I-AA with a bang.

The Thundering Herd would step up to Division I-A the following season, but they had unfinished business to attend to first. After winning the national championship in 1992, they'd been on the brink of doing so again three times, only to fall short twice in the finals and once in the semifinals.

Most recently, in 1995, they'd dropped a heartbreaker to Montana in the championship game, losing 22-20 by the margin of a single safety.

When the same two teams met in '96, it wasn't just a rematch, it was a matchup of two unbeaten teams.

This year's Marshall team was led by a freshman receiver named Randy Moss, who would later excel with the NFL's Minnesota Vikings. Moss set records for receiving yards and touchdowns by a freshman, and bested Jerry Rice's mark by catching a touchdown pass in 11 consecutive games.

Quarterback Eric Kresser had a similarly stellar season, tying a school record with 35 touchdown passes, and Bob Pruett was named national coach of the year in his first season at Marshall. But none of that meant anything to an unbeaten Montana team that came in ranked No. 1.

Montana and Marshall had both run the table through 14 games, and when they met Dec. 21 at Marshall University Stadium in Huntington, something had to give.

It wouldn't be Marshall.

The Thundering Herd, who came into the game ranked second in the nation, roared out to a 23-0 lead and never looked back against the top-ranked Grizzlies. Less than a minute into the fourth quarter, the scoreboard read 46-6, and Montana had yet to reach the end zone.

The Grizzlies managed to make it look closer than it was by scoring 23 points in the fourth quarter, falling 49-29. But there was no doubt in anyone's mind who the best Division I-AA team was in 1996.

There was no doubt about something else, as well.

Marshall was ready for the big time.

Softball

Huntington High won the state AAA softball championship.

1997

Football

Playing its first season Division I-A, Marshall set a record for the best debut at that level with 10 wins, beating Toledo 34-14 for the Mid-American Conference championship.

Sophomore quarterback Chad Pennington led the nation in touchdown passes with 39, and Randy Moss won the Biletnikoff

Award as the nation's outstanding receiver. He was also a Heisman Trophy finalist.

Music

A pair of classic rock acts, Cheap Trick and Quiet Riot, plugged in their amps and Coyote's Wild Dawg Saloon on 3rd Avenue.

1998

Baseball

After three years without a baseball team, Huntington had one again when the Rail Kings came to town, playing in the independent Heartland League, which was in its third season.

The league started the season with six teams, but Huntington and Booneville, Mississippi, both folded midway through. And when the Cook County Cheetahs bolted for another league, the Heartland League closed up shop, as well.

The Rail Kings, who had played in Altoona, Pennsylvania, the previous season, wound up their abbreviated history in Huntington with a less-than-stellar 9-23 record.

Football

Marshall rolled through the 1998 college football season with just a single loss in 13 games: a 34-13 upset at Bowling Green. But victories of 24-21 over South Carolina in the season's third week 23-17 over Toledo in the conference championship game punctuated a hugely successful year.

A 48-29 triumph over Louisville in the Motor City Bowl — the school's first-ever bowl triumph — put an exclamation point on the season, which turned out to be just a warmup for an even more successful year in 1999.

Quarterback Chad Pennington threw for 3,830 yards and 28

touchdowns with just seven interceptions on the year.

He would go on to play 11 NFL seasons, eight of them with the New York Jets, and was the only player to win Comeback Player of the Year honors twice (in 2002 and 2008). When he retired in 2010, he was the NFL's all-time leader in completion percentage at 66 percent, a figure since surpassed by Drew Brees.

1999

Marshall quarterback Chad Pennington signs a football in 2003 as a member of the New York Jets. *Public domain*

Football

Marshall had its most successful football season ever, finishing the year undefeated in 13 games, including a 21-3 victory over Brigham Young in the Motor City Bowl.

The Thundering Herd opened its season with a 13-10 triumph over Clemson of the Atlantic Coast Conference, then followed that up with a 63-3 throttling of Liberty University. They ran through their Mid-American Conference schedule with only a single competitive contest: a 34-30 win over Western Michigan in the championship game.

For the season, Marshall scored 463 points for an average of 35.6 a game while giving up just 137. Quarterback Chad Pennington was a Heisman Trophy finalist after completing 68 percent of his passes for 3,799 yards and 37 touchdowns with just 11 interceptions.

The season capped a four-year stretch in which Marshall won 50 games and lost just four, including a 25-1 record in 1998 and '99. The program was the winningest of any in Division I during the nineties, with a record of 114-25 during the decade.

One of the spires from the 6th Street Bridge, preserved downtown. *Author photo*

This Sunoco sign on U.S. 60 is one of the largest you're likely to see.
Author photo

Looking down 4th Avenue at the Keith-Albee Theatre and the West Virginia
Building. *Author photo*

A pink-and-green giraffe greets travelers on U.S. 60 on the way into town. *Author photo*

Coca-Cola bottling plant on 3rd Avenue. *Author photo*

A vintage gas station just off U.S. 60 in Huntington. *Author photo*

References

"9 False Arrest Suits Entered," Raleigh Register, Beckley, W.Va., p. 3, Jan. 12, 1962.

"25 Things We Miss Most," huntingtonquarterly.com.

"100 Blue Law Indictments To Be Sought," Beckley Post-Herald, p. 2, Feb. 11, 1962.

"2011-12 Marshall Men's Basketball Media Guide," issuu.com, Nov. 9, 2011.

"$7,000 In Loot," Beckley Post-Herald, p. 1, May 27, 1963.

"15,000 Hail Marshall Champs," Minneapolis Morning Tribune, p. 20, March 17, 1947.

"$362,000 Fire at Huntington," Lexington Leader, p. 7, July 14, 1919.

"1,500,000 Is Loss In Huntington Blaze After Gas Explosion," Cincinnati Enquirer, p. 6, Oct. 22, 1950.

Abbess, Stephanie and Adkins, Joan. "Huntington's Olympic Pool (1954-2006)," theclio.com, Dec. 12, 2017.

Alexandersen, Christian. "Tri-State remembers Soupy," herald-dispatch.com, Oct. 23, 2009.

"The Anderson-Newcomb Co.," Big Sandy News (Louisa, Ky.), p. 1, Jan. 18, 1907.

"Another in Wave Of Major Fires Hits Huntington," Newark (Ohio) Advocate, p. 9, March 10, 1953.

"Automobile Row," cabellcountydoorstothepast.com.

Brammer, Emily and Emma Satterfield. "Sam's Hot Dog Stand," theclio.com, May 5, 2020.

Ben M. and Satterfield, Emma. "Heiner's Bakery," theclio.com, Nov. 13, 2019.

Betz, Shelly and Lee, Rick. "Local Charm," huntingtonquarterly.com.

"Billy Ray Cyrus" (search), rolandnote.com.

"Bob Byrd's LP Is a Hit With the Homefolks," Lexington Herald, p. 30, Dec. 22, 1978.

Box Office, yumpyu.com, Jan. 17, 1966.

Bowen, Tristan. "Huntington Flood Wall," theclio.com, Feb. 3, 2020.

Braun, Saul. "The Transmogrification of Soupy Sales," classic.esquire.com, Oct. 1, 1967.

Bridgehunter.com.

Bryant, Brooks. "The Strip: Prohibition and Bootlegging in Huntington," theclio.com, Oct. 29, 2019.

Bryant, Brooks. "Ritter Park," theclio.com, Feb. 11, 2021.

Buell, Stephen David. "The History and Development of WSAZ-TV, Channel 3, Huntington, West Virginia," the Ohio State University, Ph.D., etd.ohiolink.edu, 1962.

"Byrd dedicates Ohio River bridge," Newark (Ohio) Advocate, p. 7, Nov. 6, 1994.

"Cabell County Courthouse," theclio.com.

"Cam Henderson Center," theclio.com, Feb. 12, 2020.

Camden Park notice, Point Pleasant Weekly Register, p. 1, May 23, 1906.

"Carnegie Public Library," West Virginia Explorer, wvexplorer.com.

Cartwright, Al. "Delaware," Wilmington Morning News, p. 3, March 5, 1978.

Casto, James E. "Fairfield" (pdf), jimcasto.com.

    "A&P Stores," herald-dispatch.com, May 30, 2016.

    "The Advertiser," herald-dispatch.com, Oct. 29, 2019.

    "Amsbary's," herald-dispatch.com, April 20, 2015.

    "Anderson-Newcomb Co.," herald-dispatch.com, Jan. 9, 2017.

    "Arena Gardens," herald-dispatch.com, March 3, 2020.

    "Big Bear Supermarkets," herald-dispatch.com, July 13, 2015.

    "Bradshaw-Diehl," herald-dispatch.com, May 19, 2014.

    "Children's Hospital," herald-dispatch.com, Nov. 17, 2020.

    "Cruise Avenue," herald-dispatch.com, June 22, 2021.

    "Davidson's Record Shop," herald-dispatch.com, Aug. 21, 2021.

    "Early Movie Houses," herald-dispatch.com, Sept. 8, 2020.

    "East Hills Mall," herald-dispatch.com, July 8, 2019.

    "First Douglass School," herald-dispatch.com, Aug. 18, 2014.

    "The five and dimes," herald-dispatch.com, Sept. 28, 2015.

    "The Gateway Hotel," herald-dispatch.com, Feb. 9, 2015.

    "Harts Family Centers," herald-dispatch.com, Dec. 8, 2020.

    "The Hotel Prichard," herald-dispatch.com, Oct. 11, 2016.

    "Huntington East High School," herald-dispatch.com, Sept. 7, 2015.

    "The Lake at Ritter Park," herald-dispatch.com, Dec. 29, 2013.

    "Miss USA Pageant," herald-dispatch.com, Nov. 24, 2020.

    "Nasser's Department Store," apnews.com, Dec. 3, 2018.

    "The Orpheum Theater," herald-dispatch.com, Oct. 11, 2016.

    "The Parkettes," herald-dispatch.com, Aug. 4, 2020.

    "The Pied Piper," herald-dispatch.com, Aug. 13, 2019.

    "Riverside Club," herald-dispatch.com, Aug. 18, 2020.

    "Sears, Roebuck & Co.," herald-dispatch.com, May 18, 2015.

    "The second city hall," herald-dispatch.com, Oct. 12, 2015.

    "Shoney's," apnews.com, June 12, 2018.

    "Stone Lodge Motel," herald-dispatch.com, Oct. 8, 2019.

"The Style Shop," herald-dispatch.com, July 6, 2021.

"The Superblock," herald-dispatch.com, July 6, 2021.

"The UpTowner Inn," herald-dispatch.com, Nov. 16, 2015.

"W.T. Grant Co.," herald-dispatch.com, May 15, 2017.

"Whiz Discount Stores," herald-dispatch.com, March 5, 2018.

"Zenner-Bradshaw Co.," herald-dispatch.com, July 11, 2016.

"Catawba Stops Marshall by 7-0," Charlotte Observer, p. 12-B, Jan. 2, 1948.

"Charters," Clarksburg Daily Telegram, p.3, Sept. 18, 1912.

"Christmas Comes To U.S.," Beckley Post-Herald, p. 20, Dec. 25, 1961.

"Cigarette Pictures," Point Pleasant Register, p. 8, June 2, 1910.

Cinematreasures.org.

"The City of Huntington Ferryboat," cabellcountydoorstothepast.com.

Cole, Merle T. "The Revenooers Enforcing Prohibition in West Virginia," wvculture.org (archived).

"Collis P. Huntington Statue," theclio.com, Aug. 10, 2021.

"Commits Suicide," Hinton Daily News, p. 2, April 1, 1913.

Conkolene "Bunny" Gray obituary, Hall Funeral Home and Crematory, Proctorville, Ohio, 2004.

"The Contest of the Century," mywvhome.com.

Craft, Candyce. "Ona Speedway," theclio.com, Dec. 12, 2018.

Cream concert ad, Huntington Advertiser, April 28, 1968.

"Cross Currents," Cincinnati Enquirer, p. 16, July 2, 1962.

Dennison, Corey F. "WSAZ Radio: 'The Worst Station from A to Z,"
        wvculture.org/goldenseal/Winter01/wsaz.html.

Deardorff-Sisler ad, Big Sandy News (Louisa, Ky.), p. 7, Nov. 1, 1912.

Deardorff-Sisler ad, Big Sandy News (Louisa, Ky.), p. 5, April 6, 1917.

"Dog Racing Banned," Cincinnati Enquirer, p. 17, May 29, 1927.

Dollar Day ad for Huntington merchants, Big Sandy News (Louisa, Ky.), p. 8, Aug. 24, 1917.

"Don and Mabel Garrison," Hinton Daily News, p. 4, Oct. 3, 1917.

Dukes, Billy. "Billy Ray Cyrus recalls hearing 'Achy Breaky Heart' for the first time,"
        tasteofcountry.com, May 5, 2017.

" 'Dutch' Nazel Dies At 86," Raleigh Register, p. 9, Oct. 28, 1969.

"East Hills Mall," abandonedonline.net.

"Electro-Metallurgical Co'.s Annual Picnic Set For Huntington July 10," Hinton Daily News, p. 8,
        July 8, 1948.

"End Of Hard-Luck Era Appeared... Then Tragedy," Beckley Post-Herald, p. 3, Nov. 16, 1970.

"Fast-Moving Music Set For Rock Fest Friday," Charleston Daily Mail, p. 15, June 10, 1970.

Ferrell, Jennifer. "Bailey's Cafeteria; 1963 Civil Rights Sit-In," theclio.com, April 20, 2020.

"Firemen Get Into the Act," Dayton Daily News, p. 8, June 15, 1988.

"Flats on 4th demolished," wsaz.com, Sept. 21, 2018.

"Floodwall History," huntingtonquarterly.com.

"For Each Death: A Personal Story," Charleston Daily Mail, p. 2, Nov. 17, 1970.

Fox, Aaron-Michael. "These 17 Photos Show How Bad The 1937 Flood Was,"
        downtownhuntington.net.

"Frostop Drive-Ins," frostop.com.

"Greenup County's Billy Ray Cyrus," countrymusichighway.com.

Groceteria.com.

Haas, Richard. "Business And Its People," Charleston Daily Mail, p. 7B, Oct. 26, 1973.

"Hal Greer, the first black player in Marshall University..." upi.com, Feb. 20, 1982.

Hanna, George. "Marshall Student's Life Spent Fighting Racial Barriers," Charleston Daily Mail, p. 4, Aug. 8, 1963.

Hanna, George. "Now They're Worrying About Respect For Law In W.Va.; It Says So Right Here; No Kiddin'!" Becklye Post-Hearald, p. 6, Dec. 16, 1962.

Hardiman, Jean. "Big Sandy Superstore Arena," theclio.com, April 6, 2017.

Harris, Jeremy et. al. "Huntington West Virginia World War I Memorial Arch," theclio.com, Nov. 18, 2020.

Hartwig, Walter. "The vintage years," Tucson Citizen, p. 16, March 12, 1983.

"Having a blast," Owensboro (Ky.) Messenger-Inquirer, p. 3, Feb. 4, 1995.

"History," cabellhuntington.com.

"History of Cabell County," cabellcounty.org.

"The History of Jim's," jimsspaghetti.com.

"Hockey Back In Huntington After 15 Year Absence," Beckley Post-Herald, p. 16, Oct.7, 1956.

Horn, Hailey. "The Guaranty Bank Building," theclio.com, Oct. 16, 2019.

"Harris Riverfront Park," theclio.com, Nov. 3, 2016.

"Old Fairfield Stadium," theclio.com, Feb. 18, 2020.

"Huntington Blizzard Statistics and History," hockeydb.com.

"Huntington Bridge," Hinton Independent-Herald, p. 3, Sept. 23, 1926.

"Huntington City Hall," theclio.com, Aug. 15, 2019.

"Huntington Fire Worst On Record," p. 8C, Oct. 22, 1950.

"Huntington Has 24 New Lanes," Sunday Gazette-Mail, p. 5D, Dec. 27, 1959.

"Huntington Has $500,000 Blaze," Hinton Leader, p. 4, Feb. 17, 1944.

"Huntington Has $1 Million Fire," "Huntington Has Heavy Fire Loss," Marysville (Ohio) Tribune, p. 1, Dec. 16, 1925.

"Huntington Hornets Statistics and History," Hockeydb.com.

"Huntington Hotels of Yesteryear," huntingtonquarterly.com.

"Huntington Loss May be a Million," Hinton Daily News, p. 1, April 2, 1913.

"Huntington Mall Facts for Kids," kids.kiddle.co.

"Huntington's Mall Contract Signed," Charleston Daily Mail, p. 7B, Jan. 5, 1973.

"Huntington Theatre Manager Is Fined," Hinton Leader, p. 7, June 20, 1929.

"Huntington Tobacco Factory to be Built," Hinton Daily News, p. 1, Dec. 15, 1917.

"Huntington, West Va. Hit By Costly Blaze," Lebanon (Pa.) Daily News, p. 10, Oct. 23, 1950.

"Huntington's Favorite Former Eateries, Part 1," huntingtonquarerly.com.

"Jim's Steak and Spaghetti House: PBS Documentary," youtube.com, April 23, 2012.

"John Moore Will Resume Duties as Swimming Teacher," Connellsville (Pa.) Daily Courier, p. 8, April 27, 1931.

Johnson, Shauna. "Huntington restaurant marks 60 years as a family-owned business," wvmetronews.com, May 27, 2019.

"Keep Dog Tracks Out," Hinton Daily News, p. 4, Oct. 5, 1935.

"Kennedy-Humphrey Race Not Only One In State," Beckley Post-Herald, p. 14, April 17, 1960.

Klein, Christopher. "8 Things You May Not Know About West Virginia," history.com, Sept. 1, 2018.

"LaPlace Frostop" blog, laplacefrostop.blogspot.com.

"League Baseball in Huntington," Charleston Advocate, p. 4, Sept. 23, 1909.

"LI Girl 2d in Beauty Test," Hempstead Newsday, p. 24, Aug. 28, 1961.

"Little Progress in Clearing Bridge Wreck," Hinton Daily News, p. 1, Jan. 2, 1913.

"Long-awaited bridge connects two states," Paducah (Ky.) Sun, p. 6, Nov. 3, 1987.

"Long's Parkette/Long's Family Restaurant," timlong.com.

"Lost Huntington: Barnett Hospital," herald-dispatch.com, Oct. 19, 2014.

"The Lost Statue," theclio.com, July 23, 2020.

"Marshall College Has First Negro on It's (sic) Basketball Team Now," Hinton Daily News, p. 6,
    Nov. 23, 1955.

"Marshall Football History," 2008 Football Guide, s3.amazonaws.com.

"Marshall Nips Hamline 55-54 in Feature of NAIB Tourney," Mason City (Iowa) Globe-Gazette, p. 17,
    March 13, 1947.

"Marshall Plane Crash Probed," Weirton Daily Times, p. 1, Nov. 16, 1970.

"Marshall Students Stage Racial Sit-in," Hinton Daily News, p. 8, July 22, 1963.

"Marshall Takes NAIB Title After Defeating Mankato College 73-59," Mason City (Iowa)
    Globe-Gazette, p. 11, March 17, 1947.

McKnight, Kyle and Satterfield, Emma. "The Simms School," theclio.com, Nov. 18, 2019.

Mead, Andy. "The Last Picture Show," Lexington Herald-Leader, p. B1, Sept. 7, 1981.

Meadows, Donald. "Lorenzen Kisses Rail But Still Wins Mountaineer 300," Raleigh Register, p. 8,
    Aug. 19, 1963.

Meadows, Donald. "Race Tickets Now On Sale," Raleigh Register, p. 6, Aug. 2, 1963.

Miller, Rikki. "The Creation and Cultural Significance of the Barnett Hospital," marshall.edu.

"New Lanes Set for Huntington," Sunday Gazette-Mail, p. 7D, Sept. 27, 1959.

"New Record of Growth Mae by Bus Company During Year," Charleston Daily Mail, p. 4, Feb. 8, 1931.

"Northcott Hall (Northcott Science Hall)," mds.marshall.edu.

"Obituary for William S. (Bill) Spurlock," chapmans-mortuary.com.

"Our Heritage," roccosristorante.com.

"Our History," camdenpark.com (archived).

Parkette ad, Charleston Daily Mail, p. 10, Feb. 11, 1951.

Parkette ad, Charleston Daily Mail, p. 27, Feb. 7, 1952.

Perry, Buddy. "Devils Toppled By Tall Express, Minutemen Beaten," Beckley Post-Herald, p. 1,
    March 23, 1969.

"Plane crash devastates Marshall University football team," history.com.

Platania, Joseph. "Sunset Cinemas," huntingtonquarterly.com.

"Pretty Teacher Is Married Price In 24 Hours After Meeting 'Fate,'" Fairmont West Virginian, p. 3,
    Aug. 1, 1913.

Price, Rachel. "These 9 Horrifying Places in West Virginia May Haunt Your Dreams,"
    onlyinyourstate.com, Sept. 16, 2021.

"Racial Protests Continue To Stir Huntington," Weirdon Daily Times, p. 1, Aug. 5, 1963.

Racing-reference.info.

"Rae Samuels Finds the Theatre Is Coming Back Into Own," Hinton Daily News, p. 3, Oct. 16, 1930.

"Remember When? Dreamland Pool," herald-dispatch.com, Aug. 6, 2011.

"Ritter Park," ghprd.org.

Robinson, Delmer. "Mountain Menus Can Be Terrific," Sunday Gazette-Mail, p. 8V, May 23, 1976.

"Roof Collapse at Auditorium Causes Death of Lt. Hensley," Huntington Advertiser, April 8, 1945,
    gendisasters.com.

"Rose Native Named Mayor of Huntington," Rochester Democrat and Chronicle, p. 8, Feb. 7, 1932.

Salvatore, John. "The Huntington Hot Dog," roadsidepeek.com.

"Sam's Hot Dog Stand," samshotdogs.com.

"Sam Snead Walks Off With Home State Open Title," Orangeburg (S.C.), Times and Democrat, p. 6, Aug. 25, 1949.

Sanders, Ralph W. "Miss USA Anxious to Retire," Decatur Daily Review, p. 12, July 11, 1962.

Satterfield, Emma. "Cam's Ham," theclio.com, April 30, 2020.

    "Dwight's Drive-In (1963-2003)," theclio.com, May 19, 2020.

    "The Fifth Avenue Hotel (1910-1980s)," theclio.com, May 15, 2020.

    "Frank's Sandwich Shop (1964-1990s)," theclio.com, April 22, 2020.

    "The French Tavern (1924-1980)," theclio.com, June 16, 2020.

    "The Gideon Building," theclio.com, June 4, 2020.

    "Midway Drive-In," theclio.com, June 11, 2020.

    "The Peanut Shoppe (1924-2009)," theclio.com, May 12, 2020.

    "Rebels and Redcoats Tavern (1959-2018)," theclio.com, June 19, 2020.

    "Ward's Do-Nuts (1947-2000)," theclio.com, July 12, 2020.

    "Wiggins Bar-B-Q (1950s-1980s)," theclio.com, April 20, 2020.

Satterfield, Emma; Pittinger, David; and Isaacs, David. "Greyhound Station – Huntington, West Virginia," theclio.com, June 30, 2020.

"Say Amendment is Constitutional," Hinton Daily News, p. 1, Nov, 11, 1912.

"Scholarship established for Huntington icon," marshall.edu, Oct. 14, 2020.

"Sit-in at the White Pantry, 1963," theclio.com, May 5, 2020.

"The Spooning Season," Fairmont West Virginian, p. 4, June 12, 1914.

Sports-reference.com.

"State Capital Notes," Fairmont West Virginian, p. 4, July 12, 1909.

Statscrew.com.

"Stewart's Original Hot Dogs 'The Little Orange Drive-In That Could," stewartshotdogs.com.

Straley, Steven Cody. "Ceredo Plaza (Former Ceredo Dog Track)," theclio.com, Sept. 3, 2018.

Straley, Steven Cody. "Guyandotte Bridge Disaster," theclio.com, Aug. 1, 2019.

"Suits Filed By Raided 'Blue Law' Workers," Raleigh Register, p. 11, Dec. 14, 1961.

Tabler, Dave. "The flood that convinced Huntington to build a flood wall," appalachianhistory.net, March 5, 2015.

"Ten Prisoners Taken in Huntington Raids," Bluefield Daily Telegraph, p. 1, Feb. 1, 1925.

Thompson, Robert. "Ceredo dog track had short, profitable life," Wayne County News, July 18, 2018.

"Tickets On Sale For Ona's '300'," Charleston Daily Mail, p. 4, July 22, 1963.

"Timeline of major events in The Herald-Dispatch's history," apnews.com, Jan. 17, 2019.

Tinubu, Aramide. "Movie Theaters and Cinema Through The Decades," cheatsheet.com, Aug. 10, 2018.

"Top Stock Car Money Winner In W. Va. Event," Weirton Daily Times, p. 8, Aug. 12, 1963.

"Topic: Drive-In Theatre – Parking Ramp Height?" film-tech.com, Jan. 7, 2003.

"Uptowner Inn Conversion to TownePlace Suites in Parkersburg, West Virginia," llwarchitects.com, June 9, 2021.

"U.S. Helps City Buy Swim Pool," p. 3, May 30, 1973.

"Ward's Do-Nuts (1947-2000)," theclio.com.

"West Virginia Under Dry Law," Fairmont West Virginian, p. 7, July 1, 1914.

"White Pantry Again Scene Of Demonstration," Beckley Post-Herald, p. 1, Aug. 11, 1963.

Wright, Katie. "Huntington Elks Lodge 313 (1909-2017)," theclio.com, June 7, 2019.

Also by the author

Historical nonfiction
Yesterday's Highways

America's First Highways

Highways of the South

The Great American Shopping Experience

Martinsville Memories

Fresno Growing Up

Danville Century

Fresno Century

Roanoke Century

San Luis Obispo Century

Cambria Century

Danville Century

Highway 99: The History of California's Main Street

Highway 101: The History of El Camino Real

The Legend of Molly Bolin

A Whole Different League

Fiction
The Talismans of Time

Pathfinder of Destiny

Nightmare's Eve

Death's Doorstep

Memortality

Paralucidity

The Only Dragon

Identity Break

Praise for other works

"If you have any interest in highways, old diners and motels and such, or 20th century US history, this book is for you. It is without a doubt one of the best highway books ever published."

— Dan R. Young, founder OLD HIGHWAY 101 group, on **Yesterday's Highways**

"Profusely illustrated throughout, **Highway 99** is unreservedly recommended as an essential and core addition to every community and academic library's California History collections."

— California Bookwatch

"... an engaging narrative that pulls the reader into the story and onto the road. ... I highly recommend **Highway 99: The History of California's Main Street**, whether you're a roadside archaeology nut or just someone who enjoys a ripping story peppered with vintage photographs."

— Barbara Gossett,
Society for Commercial Archaeology Journal

"The genres in this volume span horror, fantasy, and science-fiction, and each is handled deftly. ... **Nightmare's Eve** should be on your reading list. The stories are at the intersection of nightmare and lucid dreaming, up ahead a signpost ... next stop, your reading pile. Keep the nightlight on."

— R.B. Payne, Cemetery Dance

"As informed and informative as it is entertaining and absorbing, **Fresno Growing Up** is very highly recommended for personal, community, and academic library 20th Century American History collections."

— John Burroughs, Reviewer's Bookwatch

"An essential primer for anyone seeking an entrée into the genre. Provost serves up a smorgasbord of highlights gleaned from his personal memories of and research into the various nooks and crannies of what 'used-to-be' in professional team sports."

— Tim Hanlon, Good Seats Still Available,
on **A Whole Different League**

"The complex idea of mixing morality and mortality is a fresh twist on the human condition. ... **Memortality** is one of those books that will incite more questions than it answers. And for fandom, that's a good thing."

— Ricky L. Brown, Amazing Stories

"Punchy and fast paced, **Memortality** reads like a graphic novel. ... (Provost's) style makes the trippy landscapes and mind-bending plot points more believable and adds a thrilling edge to this vivid crossover fantasy."

— Foreword Reviews

"**Memortality** by Stephen Provost is a highly original, thrilling novel unlike anything else out there."

— David McAfee, bestselling author of
33 A.D., 61 A.D., and 79 A.D.

"Provost sticks mostly to the classics: vampires, ghosts, aliens, and even dragons. But trekking familiar terrain allows the author to subvert readers' expectations. ... Provost's poetry skillfully displays the same somber themes as the stories. ... Worthy tales that prove external forces are no more terrifying than what's inside people's heads."

— Kirkus Reviews on **Nightmare's Eve**

About the author

Stephen H. Provost is the author of several books on 20th century America, covering topics that range from his hometown to department stores and shopping centers; from pop music and sports icons to the history of our nation's highways. During a 30-year career in journalism, he worked as a managing editor, sports editor, copy desk chief, columnist and reporter at five newspapers. As a novelist, he has written about dragons, mutant superheroes, and things that go bump in the night. A California native, he now lives in Virginia.

Did you enjoy this book?

Recommend it to a friend. And please consider rating it and/or leaving a brief review online at Amazon, Barnes & Noble and Goodreads.

Made in the USA
Middletown, DE
24 January 2022

59530544R00113